SRA **Specific Skill Series**
for Reading

Making Inferences

Sixth Edition

SRA

Columbus, OH

The **McGraw·Hill** Companies

Cover: © Photodisc/Getty Images, Inc.

SRAonline.com

Mc Graw Hill **SRA**

Send all inquiries to:
SRA/McGraw-Hill
8787 Orion Place
Columbus, OH 43240-4027

ISBN 0-07-604071-2

1 2 3 4 5 6 7 8 9 BCH 12 11 10 09 08 07 06 05

PURPOSE:

MAKING INFERENCES is designed to develop one of the most difficult interpretive skills—arriving at a *probable* conclusion from a limited amount of information. **MAKING INFERENCES** requires students to *read between the lines.* They must utilize previously acquired knowledge and past experiences in order to fully comprehend the message of the text.

FOR WHOM:

The skill of **MAKING INFERENCES** is developed through a series of books spanning ten levels (Picture, Preparatory, A, B, C, D, E, F, G, H). The Picture Level is for students who have not acquired a basic sight vocabulary. The Preparatory Level is for students who have a basic sight vocabulary but are not yet ready for the first-grade-level book. Books A through H are appropriate for students who can read on levels one through eight, respectively.

THE NEW EDITION:

The sixth edition of the *Specific Skill Series for Reading* maintains the quality and focus that has distinguished this program for more than 40 years. A key element central to the program's success has been the unique nature of the reading selections. Fiction and nonfiction pieces about current topics have been designed to stimulate the interest of students, motivating them to use the comprehension strategies they have learned to further their reading. To keep this important aspect of the program intact, a percentage of the reading selections has been replaced in order to ensure the continued relevance of the subject material.

In addition, a significant percentage of the artwork in the program has been replaced to give the books a contemporary look. The cover photographs are designed to appeal to readers of all ages.

SESSIONS:

Short practice sessions are the most effective. It is desirable to have a practice session every day or every other day, using a few units each session.

SCORING:

Students should record their answers on the reproducible worksheets. The worksheets make scoring easier and provide uniform records of the students' work. Using worksheets also avoids consuming the exercise books.

It is important for students to know how well they are doing. For this reason, units should be scored as soon as they have been completed. Then a discussion can be held in which students justify their choices. (The *Language Activity Pages,* many of which are open-ended, do not lend themselves to an objective score; thus there are no answer keys for these pages.)

GENERAL INFORMATION ON *MAKING INFERENCES:*

The difference between a *conclusion* and an *inference,* as presented in this series, is that a conclusion is a logical deduction based upon conclusive evidence, while an inference is an "educated guess" based upon evidence that is less than conclusive. Read this sample:

> Captain Fujihara quickly parked the fire truck, grabbed his helmet, and rushed into the house at 615 Oak Street.

You can *conclude* that Captain Fujihara knows how to drive because that ability was required to park the fire truck. You can *infer* that there is a fire at 615 Oak Street because Captain Fujihara took his helmet and rushed into that house. This is an inference because firefighters do rush to put out fires. It is an inference because there might be another reason for the firefighter's rushing to the house. Captain Fujihara might live there and be late for supper. Thus, an inference is supported by evidence, but the evidence is not necessarily conclusive.

SUGGESTED STEPS:

1. Students read the text. After reading, students examine the statements that follow the text to determine whether each is a factually true statement (T), a false statement (F), or a valid inference (I). ("True" statements are those about which the reader can be *certain* from the text.)

2. Then students reexamine the text for evidence to support their decisions.

3. Students record their answers on the worksheets.

RELATED MATERIALS:

Specific Skill Series Assessment Book provides the teacher with a pretest and a posttest for each skill at each grade level. These tests will help the teacher assess the students' performance in each of the nine comprehension skills.

In a story a writer does not tell the reader everything. A careful reader is able to make educated guesses about things the author does not tell. An educated guess is a guess that is based on facts the author provides plus the reader's own knowledge and experience. For example, an author may write the following in a story.

> Noah clutched a handkerchief tightly in his fingers. Sobbing, he raised his hand to wipe away the tears that trickled down his cheeks.

You can make an educated guess that Noah is sad, based on the fact that he is crying and on your own knowledge that people sometimes cry when they are sad.

This kind of educated guess is called an **inference.** You cannot be certain that your inference is correct. In the example above, Noah may be crying because he has hurt himself. Or he may be crying because he is very happy. Other details in the story will help you make the best possible guess.

In this book you will read short stories. Then you will read four sentences about each story. You will have to decide whether each sentence is true (T), false (F), or an inference (I). A true statement tells a fact from the story. A false statement is one that is not true. An inference says something that is *probably* true based on facts in the story and your own knowledge and experience. More than one sentence about one story may be true, false, or an inference. You must read each sentence carefully to decide which it is.

1.   "Have you ever heard someone call their hair their 'crowning glory'?" asked Jessica.

"No, but I do like to have my hair looking a certain way," said Olivia.

"Hair actually has a very important function," said Jessica. "It protects our heads from bumps and bruises and even keeps us warmer in winter."

"The hair on the rest of the body doesn't seem that important," commented Olivia.

"That hair also has a purpose. Our eyelashes screen out dust and other tiny objects that might fly into our eyes. Our eyebrows cushion our eyes and prevent sweat from dripping down into them."

2.   Once upon a time, a wolf lay on the ground, recovering from an injury. He saw a sheep passing by and cried out to her, "Good stranger, would you bring me some water? I could probably get some meat for myself, if only I could have some water!"

The sheep pondered, then replied, "I will not, for I can see that if I brought you the water, you would have *no* trouble getting the meat!"

3.   Ms. Rollins's voice shook a little as she gave the students their assignment for the period. She wasn't used to teaching seventh and eighth graders. Most of the time she worked with younger students, and this group of teenagers made her a little nervous. They looked so grown up, and the work they were doing was quite advanced. But she knew Mr. Andrews well. *What he would do, I'll do,* she thought.

4.   Pedro had lived his entire life by the sea, having learned at his father's knee the art of sailing. Now, many years later, he was setting out on the ultimate challenge—to sail solo around the world. This voyage would provide the maximum test for Pedro. The difficult task of single-handed sailing, coupled with months of solitude, would bring many experienced sailors to their breaking point. But Pedro was determined not to be found among those victims.

5.   Thomas Alva Edison watched in expectation as his assistant, Charles Bachelor, removed the mold from the furnace. Within was the priceless filament that Edison hoped would climax his experiments. As Bachelor removed the filament, it broke. "Let's try again," Edison said. Not until three days later was an intact filament successfully mounted inside a glass bulb. Quickly the air inside the bulb was exhausted and the current turned on. The filament glowed brightly! Disregarding their 74 sleepless hours, the two experimenters watched the first electric light burn for 40 more hours.

		T	F	I
1.	(A) The hair on our heads is not important.	☐	☐	☐
	(B) Jessica knows more about the purpose of hair than Olivia.	☐	☐	☐
	(C) Eyelashes protect the eyes from dust and objects.	☐	☐	☐
	(D) The hair described as our 'crowning glory' grows on our heads.	☐	☐	☐

		T	F	I
2.	(A) The wolf planned to eat the sheep.	☐	☐	☐
	(B) The sheep thought about the wolf's request.	☐	☐	☐
	(C) The wolf was taking a nap.	☐	☐	☐
	(D) The sheep and the wolf knew each other.	☐	☐	☐

		T	F	I
3.	(A) Ms. Rollins was substituting as a teacher for Mr. Andrews.	☐	☐	☐
	(B) Ms. Rollins's voice shook a little.	☐	☐	☐
	(C) Most of the time Ms. Rollins taught high school.	☐	☐	☐
	(D) The work the students were doing was quite advanced.	☐	☐	☐

		T	F	I
4.	(A) Sailing was a new adventure for Pedro.	☐	☐	☐
	(B) Pedro intended to sail around the world by himself.	☐	☐	☐
	(C) Pedro was confident that he could achieve his goal.	☐	☐	☐
	(D) Pedro was raised far from the sea.	☐	☐	☐

		T	F	I
5.	(A) The filament was mounted successfully on the first day.	☐	☐	☐
	(B) The experimenters were patient and persistent workers.	☐	☐	☐
	(C) When the current was turned on, the filament burned brightly.	☐	☐	☐
	(D) Charles Bachelor was Thomas Edison's assistant.	☐	☐	☐

1.   Etu was still a bit nervous about his job. It was good, hard, outdoor work—the kind he liked. But he worried that he would do something wrong. Then he heard his boss's voice on the phone. "Etu, put the spruce saplings along the Clarks' property line in the back. Oh, and good job yesterday with reseeding at the Jason's." Etu smiled and relaxed.

2.   *The leaves are really colorful this year,* Carmelita thought as she walked through the park. *Grandma so liked the fall season when she was here. The trees in her Puerto Rican homeland never turn brilliant colors like these.* Carmelita continued her stroll. *I will write to Grandma soon, although not much has happened since my last letter.* Then she paused, smiled to herself, and began collecting more leaves. These were the brightest colors, the most interesting shapes. *I remember Grandma helping me make a booklet of pressed leaves once,* she reflected.

3.   This horse had never been ridden. The young newcomer, Dante, stood outside the corral, nervously watching the wild-eyed creature stomp along the inside perimeter. *We're both afraid,* Dante thought. *I can see that.* He inhaled the morning air deeply as he pulled on his new gloves. He heard the encouraging calls of the cowhands as he unlatched the gate. To gain their respect, Dante didn't have to stay on the horse long—but he had to show he could ride. "You can do it, Dante," called Che. "You're smarter than that horse."

4.   Toru's parents were in the kitchen putting dishes, pots, and pans into the various cupboards and organizing them. Half-empty boxes were scattered about the room. "How was school, Toru?" his father asked as the young boy breezed into the room.

    "Not bad!" Toru answered enthusiastically. "I ate lunch with a couple of neat guys who live on the next street, and—guess what—there's a swimming pool in the school, and they have a team too! I'm trying out for it next week!"

5.   "Who owns Antarctica?" asked Luke.

    "Nobody owns it. In 1959 twelve different countries signed the Antarctic Treaty, agreeing to share and preserve the continent," replied Angelo.

    "Wow, that's hard to believe. It seems as though it's valuable and that there would be a struggle over it," replied Luke.

    "Powerful countries such as the United Kingdom, the United States, and the former Soviet Union agreed to give up their territory claims, share research findings, and avoid military activity on the continent. Five years later they adopted a treaty that protects wildlife and designated areas," explained Angelo.

    "It is great to know that countries can cooperate," replied Luke.

1.   T F I

1. (A) Etu enjoyed working outdoors. ☐ ☐ ☐
    (B) Etu is a gardener. ☐ ☐ ☐
    (C) Etu's boss gave him instructions over the phone. ☐ ☐ ☐
    (D) Etu's boss is not pleased with his work. ☐ ☐ ☐

                                                             T F I

2. (A) Carmelita's grandmother's home is in Puerto Rico. ☐ ☐ ☐
    (B) Carmelita's grandmother had helped Carmelita. ☐ ☐ ☐
    (C) Carmelita was planning to write to her grandmother soon. ☐ ☐ ☐
    (D) Carmelita would enclose some leaves in her next letter to
         Grandma. ☐ ☐ ☐

                                                             T F I

3. (A) Dante had never ridden a wild horse before this. ☐ ☐ ☐
    (B) Che and the other cowhands offered encouragement to Dante. ☐ ☐ ☐
    (C) The other cowhands had already ridden this horse. ☐ ☐ ☐
    (D) Dante had to stay on the horse for hours to prove he could ride. ☐ ☐ ☐

                                                             T F I

4. (A) Toru had eaten lunch at home. ☐ ☐ ☐
    (B) Toru's family has just moved into a new home. ☐ ☐ ☐
    (C) There was a swimming pool in the school. ☐ ☐ ☐
    (D) Toru's parents were organizing things in the kitchen when
         Toru got home. ☐ ☐ ☐

                                                             T F I

5. (A) The Antarctic Treaty is an unusual example of cooperation. ☐ ☐ ☐
    (B) Antarctica is divided into 12 different sections. ☐ ☐ ☐
    (C) Before the treaty, different countries had claims of territory. ☐ ☐ ☐
    (D) The Antarctic Treaty was signed in 1959. ☐ ☐ ☐

1. "I just read about a Cherokee man who invented a system of 'talking leaves' in the late 1700s," said Lusita.

"Who was it, and what were 'talking leaves'?" asked Sean.

"It was Sequoya. He noticed that European settlers communicated with each other by way of written words, or 'talking leaves.' Sequoya then spent many years creating an alphabet of symbols. Although he faced difficulties, Sequoya was able to teach this system to the rest of the Cherokee nation," said Lusita.

2. Grandmother Duzant took the sweet-potato pudding out of the oven and placed it next to the coconut drops cooling on the kitchen counter. Chicken and shrimp gumbo and beef dumplings had already been prepared. She hoped there would be enough food to satisfy the appetites of family and friends coming to keep her company at dinner late that afternoon. She glanced once again at the calendar. *Yes,* she thought, *I have much to be thankful for.*

3. Kari placed her artwork on the display board and stepped back, critically eyeing the painting she'd worked on for so long. "I've got to win the prize money for my painting," she said to her brother Reed. "It's the only way I'll ever have enough money to buy Mom the locket. I can't wait to see her face when she opens the locket and sees the photograph," said Kari.

"She's sure to like it," said Reed. "I know she likes that photograph of our family."

4. Kareem had purchased a new ten-speed bike—a sleek, silver model it had taken him six months to pay for. Now every day after school, Kareem could be found in the garage, avidly cleaning the wheels or shining the spokes.

"Don't you have anything better to do?" questioned Jacqui. "I never clean my bike, and it looks as good as new."

Kareem couldn't help laughing as he glanced at Jacqui's bike. "If you say so," he said.

5. Lu-Chan was a very popular boy. He was friendly and fun-loving—qualities that many people liked. At school students and teachers admired him. Usually these feelings were mutual. He was extremely kind to everyone he met. This was especially evident when new students came to school. Lu-Chan would always go out of his way to make a newcomer feel welcome. No one was surprised when Lu-Chan asked Miguela to have lunch with him and his friends.

		T	F	I

1. **(A)** Sean was unfamiliar with "talking leaves." ☐ ☐ ☐
(B) The European settlers couldn't read or write. ☐ ☐ ☐
(C) Sequoya gave the Cherokees their first alphabet. ☐ ☐ ☐
(D) Sequoya used the same alphabet as the settlers. ☐ ☐ ☐

		T	F	I

2. **(A)** Coconut drops were cooling on the kitchen counter. ☐ ☐ ☐
(B) Relatives and friends were coming for lunch. ☐ ☐ ☐
(C) Grandmother Duzant lived alone. ☐ ☐ ☐
(D) It was Thanksgiving. ☐ ☐ ☐

		T	F	I

3. **(A)** Kari hopes to win a prize for her sculpture. ☐ ☐ ☐
(B) Kari worked hard on the painting. ☐ ☐ ☐
(C) Kari will probably put a family photograph in the locket for
her mom. ☐ ☐ ☐
(D) Kari's mom likes that photograph. ☐ ☐ ☐

		T	F	I

4. **(A)** Kareem kept his bike clean and shiny. ☐ ☐ ☐
(B) Jacqui cleaned her bike every day. ☐ ☐ ☐
(C) Kareem knew his bike was much cleaner than Jacqui's. ☐ ☐ ☐
(D) Jacqui said her bike looked as good as new. ☐ ☐ ☐

		T	F	I

5. **(A)** Miguela is a new student at Lu-Chan's school. ☐ ☐ ☐
(B) Lu-Chan is not on good terms with the other students. ☐ ☐ ☐
(C) New students were always made to feel welcome by Lu-Chan. ☐ ☐ ☐
(D) Everyone was surprised when Lu-Chan asked Miguela to join
him and his friends for lunch. ☐ ☐ ☐

1.   Some things improve over time. For more than 25 years, concerned citizens have been working to restore Pickering Creek. Just two decades ago, during heavy rains, the inadequate sewer systems of nearby communities would overflow and release sewage into the creek. Sewer upgrades now prevent this from happening. Scouting groups organize cleanup parties on Saturdays, removing old tires, rusted parts, and bottles from the creek. Other groups plant native trees and plants along its banks to control erosion. Now the challenge is to keep hard, unnatural surfaces out of its watershed area. Plants and natural ground absorb water, but rooftops, patios, and pavement cause runoff and flooding.

2.   African American author Maya Angelou was born Marguerite Johnson in St. Louis, Missouri, in 1928 and was brought up by her grandmother in Stamps, Arkansas. Her famous book, *I Know Why the Caged Bird Sings,* is a reflection of her own childhood and experiences growing up. Another autobiographical book by Angelou recounts her travels to Africa and her search for home. She wrote, "I knew my people had never completely left Africa. We had sung it in our blues, shouted it in our gospel, and danced the continent in our breakdowns."

3.   Concertgoers might not realize it, but the violin bow plays an important role in the orchestra. Violinists value their bows for creating rich sound. Many violinists believe it is better to have a high-quality bow and a violin of average quality than the other way around. Bows are more than just hair and wood. High-quality violin bows are crafted from wood derived from a rare Brazilian tree—the pernambuco tree. Pernambuco wood is springy, strong, and light. Professional bow makers are working hard with other groups to make sure this valuable tree species does not disappear.

4.   In Colonial Boston, teenage boys often learned trades such as silversmithing and shipbuilding by becoming apprentices. An apprentice left his family's home and moved in with a master, someone who already practiced a trade. For several years the apprentice worked for the master, learning about the trade through hands-on experience. The hours were long, and there was little time for entertainment, but the hardships were worthwhile. After apprenticeship most tradesmen were able to practice on their own.

5.   Elena looked pale as she left the telephone booth and hurried to the reservations desk with her luggage. "I must get a flight to New York as soon as possible," she said.

    "There's a flight leaving at midnight. There's one seat available," said the reservations clerk.

    "Good. I'll take it. My name is Elena Galvez. I just came off your New York to London flight but must return to New York," said Elena as she paid for her ticket. *When I get to Kennedy Airport, I'll take a taxi to the hospital,* she thought.

		T	**F**	**I**

1. **(A)** Citizens have been restoring Pickering Creek for 25 decades. ☐ ☐ ☐
(B) Pickering Creek is still in danger of flooding. ☐ ☐ ☐
(C) The work to protect Pickering Creek will continue for years to come. ☐ ☐ ☐
(D) The cleanup parties were organized by scouting groups. ☐ ☐ ☐

2. **(A)** A restrictive childhood made Maya Angelou feel like a captive bird. ☐ ☐ ☐
(B) Angelou was born in St. Louis, Missouri, in 1928. ☐ ☐ ☐
(C) One of Angelou's books is about her travels in Africa. ☐ ☐ ☐
(D) Angelou was reared in Arkansas by an aunt. ☐ ☐ ☐

3. **(A)** Pernambuco trees grow in Brazil. ☐ ☐ ☐
(B) Pernambuco wood is heavy and brittle. ☐ ☐ ☐
(C) The pernambuco tree is not abundant. ☐ ☐ ☐
(D) Violins are far more important than bows. ☐ ☐ ☐

4. **(A)** Apprentices worked for their masters for a few years. ☐ ☐ ☐
(B) Apprentices lived at home while they were learning their trade. ☐ ☐ ☐
(C) It was important for apprentices to pay close attention to what their masters said and did. ☐ ☐ ☐
(D) In Colonial Boston, many boys did not go to college. ☐ ☐ ☐

5. **(A)** It was unimportant to Elena where the seat was on the airplane. ☐ ☐ ☐
(B) Elena got a seat on a plane leaving at midnight. ☐ ☐ ☐
(C) Elena had just flown from New York to Paris. ☐ ☐ ☐
(D) Someone dear to Elena is in the hospital. ☐ ☐ ☐

1.   "Why is there a lion in our yard?" Jan asked his parents.

"Come on," said Mom and Dad. "We're trying to watch television. You know very well there's no lion in the yard."

No sooner had Jan's parents spoken these words when an announcer appeared on the television screen with a special message: "We interrupt this program to bring you word that a lion has escaped from the zoo. We repeat: A lion has escaped from the zoo!"

2.   Grace couldn't believe her good fortune. Just as her neighbor was heading out of her driveway with a bag of clothes to give away, she saw Grace. She opened her car window and asked if Grace was interested in the clothes. Grace said she would love to take a look and thanked her neighbor. At home she tried on stylish shirts, sweatshirts, and jeans. The clothes were barely worn, and most of them fit her perfectly. *It's my lucky day,* thought Grace. Then she started sneezing violently. She couldn't figure out why. It wasn't allergy season. The *Kaufmanns' cats,* she thought.

3.   Empress Josephine Bonaparte collected every known variety of rosebush from around the world to plant in her gardens at Malmaison near Paris, France. Even ships captured at sea by the French navy were searched for new species of roses. Then she commissioned the French artist Pierre Joseph Redouté to paint the 250 varieties. After Josephine's death, the property containing the exquisite rose gardens changed hands several times. Although it was largely destroyed in a battle, the beauty of Malmaison lives on.

4.   Julia promised her parents that she would improve her grades at school. "Don't worry," she said. "When the next report card comes, my grades will be higher."

For several weeks, Julia spent many evening hours in her bedroom. When the sounds of the music she played constantly were too loud, her mom asked her to lower the volume. Julia did so. But the next evening her music sounded even louder than before.

Days later, when the young student received her report card, she found that her grades had not improved at all.

5.   "I don't always like getting sweaty," said Jay.

"Why not? Perspiration is a natural way for the body to keep cool," said Shian.

"I guess during a soccer game, I do like the feeling of a breeze blowing on my damp neck," said Jay.

"Did you know that little compartments called sweat glands under the skin produce sweat and send it to the skin's surface? When perspiration covers the skin, it starts to evaporate. Evaporation, however, requires heat. It draws the needed heat from our skin, causing us to feel cooler," explained Shian.

"I guess I should appreciate perspiration," said Jay.

Unit 5

T F I

1. **(A)** A lion had escaped from the zoo. ☐ ☐ ☐
(B) At first, Mom and Dad told Jan to go back out and play. ☐ ☐ ☐
(C) Jan only imagined that he had seen a lion in the yard. ☐ ☐ ☐
(D) Mom and Dad believed Jan after they heard the television report. ☐ ☐ ☐

T F I

2. **(A)** Grace's neighbor gave her the clothes because she happened to see her. ☐ ☐ ☐
(B) The shirts, sweatshirts, and jeans fit well. ☐ ☐ ☐
(C) The clothes were out of fashion. ☐ ☐ ☐
(D) Cat hair on the clothes caused Grace's allergic reaction. ☐ ☐ ☐

T F I

3. **(A)** The beauty of Josephine's rose gardens lives on in the paintings of Redouté. ☐ ☐ ☐
(B) Josephine collected 250 species of roses for her gardens. ☐ ☐ ☐
(C) Josephine's gardens are at Versailles, France. ☐ ☐ ☐
(D) The French navy searched ships captured at sea for new species of roses. ☐ ☐ ☐

T F I

4. **(A)** The music had distracted Julia as she studied. ☐ ☐ ☐
(B) Julia told her parents not to worry about her school grades. ☐ ☐ ☐
(C) Julia's mother asked her to turn up the volume so the music could be heard. ☐ ☐ ☐
(D) The grades on Julia's report card had not improved at all. ☐ ☐ ☐

T F I

5. **(A)** Sweat glands are muscles under the skin. ☐ ☐ ☐
(B) Evaporation uses heat. ☐ ☐ ☐
(C) Jay has never felt the benefits of perspiration. ☐ ☐ ☐
(D) Shian knows more about perspiration than Jay. ☐ ☐ ☐

1.   "Are you getting ready for the World Series?" asked Elena.

"Yes, I'm listening to CDs so I can hear the difference between wood thrushes and gray-cheeked thrushes," said Drew.

"I heard you could find a yellow-billed cuckoo in the Great Swamp," said Elena.

"What on earth are you talking about?" interjected Miguel.

"We are on a team in the World Series of Birding," said Drew. "It is a 24-hour birding marathon that takes place in New Jersey. Whichever team counts the greatest number of bird species within 24 hours wins. It is very competitive, but the money we raise goes toward conservation."

2.   With his fishing pole dangling from the rack behind him, 15-year-old Kenneth pedaled his bicycle at top speed. The sky was growing increasingly dark, and the air felt heavy. "It's going to start raining," he said aloud. *Tornado weather,* he thought, pedaling faster. He had just left Murphy's Pond with his friend Manuel. Both boys were great fishermen. They were always able to catch enough fish for dinner. Today they had not caught many. Tonight's meal would be smaller than usual.

3.   "Step on the scale, Evan," said the white-coated doctor. The doctor adjusted the weights on the scale until they balanced.

"How am I doing, Dr. Chen?" asked Evan.

"Each week you do a little better," said the doctor, scribbling something on Evan's chart. "I'm going to change your medicine." The doctor wrote out a prescription and handed it to Evan. "This new protein drink should get you back up there more quickly."

4.   "I'm coming around the room to look at your homework, class," declared Mr. Moseley.

Allen's hand shot up. "May I leave the room?" he asked anxiously. "I just remembered that my mom asked me to make an important phone call."

"I'm glad you remembered," said Mr. Moseley. "It's easy to forget. So that I won't forget to check your homework, let me see it before you go to make your call."

5.   Jamal agreed to play after-school basketball with his friend Jeff at Jeff's junior high school. "I've never been to a junior high before," said Jamal. "Will they let me in?"

"No problem," said Jeff. "Try to look like a junior-high student. Just walk in as if you know your way around. The gym's right on the first floor."

The next afternoon Jamal entered the first-floor lobby of the junior high school. A teacher was standing there. "May I help you, young man?" she asked.

Unit 6

1.
- **(A)** Drew is listening to recorded bird calls.
- **(B)** Miguel has never heard of the World Series of Birding.
- **(C)** Yellow-billed cuckoos were spotted in the Great Meadow.
- **(D)** Successful birding requires skill and knowledge.

T F I

2.
- **(A)** Kenneth was 15 years old.
- **(B)** Kenneth's fishing pole was on his bicycle rack.
- **(C)** The boys left the pond early because they saw signs of a storm approaching.
- **(D)** Manuel and Kenneth had caught no fish.

T F I

3.
- **(A)** Evan wants to gain weight.
- **(B)** Evan had never been to that doctor before.
- **(C)** The doctor was wearing a white coat.
- **(D)** Evan's new medicine is a protein drink.

T F I

4.
- **(A)** Mr. Moseley asked for Allen's homework before letting him leave.
- **(B)** Allen outsmarted Mr. Moseley.
- **(C)** Mr. Moseley knew that Allen was trying to avoid having his homework checked.
- **(D)** Allen didn't really have to make a phone call.

T F I

5.
- **(A)** The gym was on the first floor.
- **(B)** The boys agreed to play football on Saturday.
- **(C)** Jeff attends the junior high.
- **(D)** Jamal did not do a convincing job of looking like a junior-high-school student.

T F I

Read the following passage about the legend of King Arthur and the Knights of the Round Table.

It is said that long ago there lived a great and noble king in the land of Britain. His name was Arthur. Arthur came to be king by drawing the magical sword Excalibur from a large rock—something that no one else had been able to do, though many had tried.

Once in power, Arthur gathered around him the bravest and strongest knights. They came together in Arthur's castle at Camelot. There they all sat at a round table, so that no one man would be at the head. Guided by the wise magician Merlin, Arthur planned how he and his knights would bring peace and prosperity to all the land.

A. Exercising Your Skill

What can you figure out about King Arthur's qualities, beliefs, and goals from what the passage tells you? Clues about characters are often revealed indirectly in stories. Often conversations, or dialogue, will help you figure out what the characters are like. Read the brief conversation below. On your paper, write one or two words or phrases to complete the statements that follow the dialogue. Your responses will be guesses based on information suggested in the passage.

"It won't be safe to enter that stronghold without help, Sire," said Gendyn. "We are clearly outnumbered."

"Thank you for your advice, Gendyn," replied Paxton. "We've come this far, though, and I don't think it's wise to leave the scroll in the hands of its captors very much longer. Our people's welfare depends on it."

One way to describe Gendyn is that he is _____.
One way to describe Paxton is that he is _____.

B. Expanding Your Skill

Rewrite the passage in Part A using information clues that would give readers a completely different idea about the personalities and values of the characters. Exchange rewritten passages with a classmate, and write new character statements like the one in Part A—that is, "One way to describe _____ is that (s)he is _____."

C. Exploring Language

Look again at the passage about King Arthur and the Knights of the Round Table. Write these headings on your paper: Directly Stated Information, Suggested Information. Now write at least ten items of directly stated information under the first heading. Such information might be: *Arthur was king long ago.* Then write at least four ideas that are hinted at indirectly in the passage. Such suggested information might be: *Many people wanted to be king.* You can guess that because Arthur became king by drawing the sword from the stone, and many others had tried to do the same thing.

D. Expressing Yourself

Choose one of these activities.

1. Choose one of the following Aesop's fables, or choose one of your favorites. Do library research if necessary to remind yourself of the details of the story. Then write a retelling of the fable. Include strong detail clues about the characters' qualities, but do not name the qualities directly. Exchange fables with a classmate. Name the qualities of each character that can be inferred, and identify the directly stated information that led to the inference. Some Aesop fables:

   "The Fox and the Grapes"
   "The Wolf in Sheep's Clothing"
   "The Goose That Laid the Golden Eggs"
   "The Shepherd Boy and the Wolf"
   "The Fox without a Tail"
   "The Hare and the Tortoise"
   "The Town Mouse and the Country Mouse"
   "The Dog and the Wolf"

2. With three or four classmates, make a skit out of one of Aesop's fables, or make up a fable of your own. Make sure the skit contains dialogue with both stated and suggested information. Perform the skit in front of a small group of classmates. After your performance ask your audience to give a description of each character's personality and goals based on what was stated or suggested in the skit.

1.   "It's time to choose parts for the class play," announced Mrs. Birns. "It helps if the character's personality matches the actor's," she continued. "Trey, I think you would be good as Romero. He's a heroic figure. And you, Miguel, would probably understand the gentleness of the character Cassio. How do you two feel about taking those roles?" she asked.

    "Sounds good," Trey and Miguel responded in unison.

    "Now, Sato," continued Mrs. Birns, "would you like the role of the comical Tenisa?"

2.   "If cider and apple juice are made from apples, why is one cloudy and the other clear?" asked Kim.

    "Cider has a cloudy, caramel look to it because it is unfiltered. It has more tiny bits of apple left in it," answered Tyrone.

    "Both juices say 'pasteurized' on the store label. What does that mean?" she asked.

    "It means the juice was heated to at least 160 degrees for six seconds. Pasteurization kills bacteria," pointed out Tyrone, "but smaller growers are not required by law to pasteurize. Some cider lovers who buy this type at roadside stands say it tastes better."

3.   Her name was Isabella, and she was born in Hurley, New York, about 1797. In her early adult years, she was a slave. After she became free, she moved to New York City but couldn't earn a good living there. In 1843 Isabella changed her name to "Sojourner Truth."

    Sojourner Truth began to travel and lecture. She became one of the greatest orators of her time. After her first few words, her audiences became spellbound. In deep though not loud tones, Sojourner Truth spoke for human rights. Her remarks were often followed by cheering.

4.   The tick is an eight-legged relative of the spider. It will attach itself to you or to your pet and suck blood. Some species carry diseases. Colorado tick fever and relapsing fever are two such diseases common in the western half of the United States. Rocky Mountain spotted fever, which occurs throughout the United States, is more serious and sometimes fatal. All three kinds of tick fever have similar symptoms that appear about a week after a tick bite: high fever, headaches, nausea, vomiting, and sometimes muscle aches. With Rocky Mountain spotted fever, tiny pink dots appear around the wrists and ankles and eventually over the entire body.

5.   Alligators have obvious adaptations that help them capture food. Their long, strong jaws filled with teeth act as powerful tools for grabbing and tearing prey. Their thrashing tails and tough hides make them strong and tough. Most people do not think of alligators as sensitive, but alligators do have a sensitive side. They have tiny bumps on their lower jaw and on part of their upper jaw. These bumps were recently discovered to be sensitive to vibrations caused by movement. Alligators spend long periods of time waiting quietly in shallow water. Their tiny bumps alert them to the movement of prey.

		T	F	I
1.	**(A)** Mrs. Birns thinks Sato has a comical personality.	☐	☐	☐
	(B) Mrs. Birns thinks an actor can play any role equally well.	☐	☐	☐
	(C) Mrs. Birns is assigning parts for the class play.	☐	☐	☐
	(D) Trey and Miguel agree with Mrs. Birns's choices for the characters of Romero and Cassio.	☐	☐	☐

		T	F	I
2.	**(A)** Unlike cider, apple juice is filtered.	☐	☐	☐
	(B) Pasteurized juice has been heated for six seconds to at least 160 degrees.	☐	☐	☐
	(C) Larger growers are required to pasteurize for safety reasons.	☐	☐	☐
	(D) Apple juice is not really made from apples.	☐	☐	☐

		T	F	I
3.	**(A)** Sojourner Truth was born in New York City.	☐	☐	☐
	(B) With only a few words, Sojourner Truth could make an audience spellbound.	☐	☐	☐
	(C) Long-continued cheering frequently followed Sojourner Truth's statements.	☐	☐	☐
	(D) Sojourner Truth gave hope to discouraged people wherever she traveled.	☐	☐	☐

		T	F	I
4.	**(A)** A person with Rocky Mountain spotted fever gets pink dots around the wrists and ankles.	☐	☐	☐
	(B) It is wise for a person who experiences nausea and vomiting following a tick bite to consult a doctor.	☐	☐	☐
	(C) A tick is a six-legged insect that carries various diseases.	☐	☐	☐
	(D) Colorado tick fever, relapsing fever, and Rocky Mountain spotted fever are three kinds of tick fever.	☐	☐	☐

		T	F	I
5.	**(A)** Alligators depend on their sensitive bumps for breathing.	☐	☐	☐
	(B) The tiny bumps are found on an alligator's lower and upper jaw.	☐	☐	☐
	(C) The bumps on an alligator's jaw are a new adaptation.	☐	☐	☐
	(D) Alligators wait for prey to come to them.	☐	☐	☐

1.   "I'd like to help you improve your handwriting, Robin," said Mrs. Torres. "I have trouble staying on the line," said Robin.

"Your letters could be formed more carefully too," replied Mrs. Torres. "You're an 'open-house' writer. It's hard to tell what some of your letters are, because you don't always close them. When you write the letter **a,** it often looks like the letter **u** or **v.**"

"Thanks, Mrs. Torres," said Robin. "I'm going to try much harder to close all my letters. I really want to make my handwriting better."

2.   The people in the neighborhood leaned from their windows and cheered the youngsters playing ball in the street below. From time to time the players stopped to let cars drive past. Some drivers were angry at the delay and honked their horns furiously. Nearby, two police officers in a patrol car sat and watched the game until one of the angry motorists approached them. "Why don't you do your job?" said the motorist. "You know it's illegal to play ball in the street."

3.   On May 5, 1930, Amy Johnson took off in a small, single-engine plane from England. She was on her way to Australia, trying to beat Bert Hinkler's record of just under 16 days for the same flight. Her plans included stops each night for rest and refueling.

One problem after another spoiled her chance of beating Hinkler's record, but she did reach Australia on May 24. It had taken her 19 days—three days longer than Hinkler. Even so, Johnson became known around the world as "Queen of the Skies."

4.   "Why do chickens contain light and dark meat, and ducks have only dark meat?" Mrs. Blackwell asked the butcher.

"Ducks fly; chickens really don't," replied the butcher. "Chickens only glide a few feet through the air."

"How does that affect the color of their meat?" asked Mrs. Blackwell.

"Birds that fly store a protein pigment in their muscles that gives them the energy to fly. This iron-containing pigment also gives the meat a darker color. Chickens have dark meat in their thighs because they use their thigh muscles for walking," said the butcher.

5.   "I must get rid of the dandelions in our lawn," said Mr. Kwan.

"I just read how nutritious they are," declared his wife. "Before you pick them, let me gather some young shoots. They contain more vitamin A than any cultivated vegetable, including carrots."

"Very interesting," said Mr. Kwan. "Please help yourself!"

"Thanks," said Mrs. Kwan. "Dandelions have as much iron as spinach and are also rich in thiamin, riboflavin, and calcium."

"In that case," replied her husband, "maybe I'll buy some dandelion seed to plant in rows near our corn, potatoes, and beans."

		T	F	I
1.	**(A)** Mrs. Torres is Robin's teacher.	☐	☐	☐
	(B) Robin has a good attitude at school.	☐	☐	☐
	(C) Mrs. Torres criticized Robin for not crossing her *t*'s.	☐	☐	☐
	(D) Mrs. Torres called Robin an "open-house" writer.	☐	☐	☐

		T	F	I
2.	**(A)** The police officers were sympathetic toward the ballplayers.	☐	☐	☐
	(B) Two motorists approached the police officers.	☐	☐	☐
	(C) The spectators encouraged the ballplayers.	☐	☐	☐
	(D) The drivers of the cars were anxious to reach their destinations.	☐	☐	☐

		T	F	I
3.	**(A)** Bert Hinkler was a well-known early aviator.	☐	☐	☐
	(B) Johnson had planned a nonstop flight from England to Australia.	☐	☐	☐
	(C) It took Johnson 19 days to fly from England to Australia.	☐	☐	☐
	(D) A single-engine plane carried Johnson from England to Australia.	☐	☐	☐

		T	F	I
4.	**(A)** Mrs. Blackwell buys chickens and ducks from the butcher.	☐	☐	☐
	(B) A pigment containing iron gives meat a darker color.	☐	☐	☐
	(C) Ducks contain only light meat.	☐	☐	☐
	(D) Chickens have dark meat only in their thighs.	☐	☐	☐

		T	F	I
5.	**(A)** Carrots contain more vitamin A than dandelions.	☐	☐	☐
	(B) Mrs. Kwan had read about the nutritional value of dandelions.	☐	☐	☐
	(C) The Kwans have a vegetable garden.	☐	☐	☐
	(D) Spinach and dandelions contain the same amount of iron.	☐	☐	☐

1.   When thinking of early electronics, not many people think of Nikola Tesla. Yet it was this Yugoslavian-born engineer who first designed a practical system for generating and transmitting alternating current for electric power. Tesla sold the rights to this invention to George Westinghouse, and he continued his own research. Tesla contributed much to the field of wireless communication as well. Ahead of his time, he even attempted wireless communication with planets other than Earth.

2.   "I can't do it," exclaimed Tyrone. "No matter how much I want to, I just can't jump from the high diving board."

Camila smiled at her friend. "Of course you can," she responded. "All you have to do is make up your mind that it's possible. The rest is easy."

Now feeling confident, Tyrone turned, climbed up the ladder, and stopped to the edge of the diving board. Then, however, in the back of his mind, he remembered what his friend Dion had said earlier.

3.   Mercedes danced rhythmically to the music as her partner, Paul, led her in the intricate steps. Both of them knew they had never really expected to attend the dance together. And they realized, also, they would probably never again go out on a date. After all, they were nothing more than acquaintances. Nevertheless, they were enjoying themselves. But when Paul looked intently across the dance floor and smiled eagerly, Mercedes followed her partner's gaze over to her friend Carol. Carol was dancing with Paul's brother.

4.   No matter how hard she looked, Mackenzie couldn't find the box of pins she needed to complete her project for school. *What will I do if I can't find them?* she thought. *I won't be able to finish on time.*

Now almost desperate, Mackenzie rushed from aisle to aisle in the small store. Sometimes she even visited the same aisle twice. She knew that if she handed her project in late, Mrs. Callacio would give her a low grade.

Then, when Mackenzie was almost ready to give up, she saw a little blue-and-red box labeled *Pins* sitting on the shelf in front of her.

5.   Serena was excited at the thought of her cousin's upcoming visit to Pennsylvania. Of course, she and Ines had known about each other for many years. But this would be the first time they would meet. "Do you think Ines will enjoy her stay with us?" she asked her mother.

Smiling, her mother said, "Of course she will. But she might have quite a few problems getting around. We'll help her as much as we can. After all, this will be the first time she'll be so far away from home."

	T	F	I
1. (A) Tesla believed that other planets were inhabited.	☐	☐	☐
(B) Tesla did not work on wireless communication.	☐	☐	☐
(C) Nikola Tesla invented a system for generating alternating electrical current.	☐	☐	☐
(D) Tesla continued his own research after he invented his alternating current system.	☐	☐	☐

	T	F	I
2. (A) Dion had discouraged Tyrone from jumping.	☐	☐	☐
(B) Tyrone felt confident after he spoke to Camila.	☐	☐	☐
(C) Camila encouraged Tyrone.	☐	☐	☐
(D) Tyrone did not want to jump from the diving board.	☐	☐	☐

	T	F	I
3. (A) Paul was interested in dancing with Carol.	☐	☐	☐
(B) Mercedes and Paul planned to go out on more dates.	☐	☐	☐
(C) Mercedes followed Paul's gaze over to Carol.	☐	☐	☐
(D) Mercedes assumed Paul's brother would be her next dancing partner.	☐	☐	☐

	T	F	I
4. (A) Mrs. Callacio is a strict teacher.	☐	☐	☐
(B) Mackenzie felt that Mrs. Callacio wouldn't mind if her project were handed in late.	☐	☐	☐
(C) The pins were in a blue-and-red box.	☐	☐	☐
(D) Mackenzie was not as observant as she could have been.	☐	☐	☐

	T	F	I
5. (A) Ines does not speak English very well.	☐	☐	☐
(B) The two girls found out about each other recently.	☐	☐	☐
(C) Serena's mother said they would help Ines get around.	☐	☐	☐
(D) Ines had been far away from home on several occasions.	☐	☐	☐

1.   Have you ever wondered if there is life on other planets? According to scientists, there could be life elsewhere in the universe, but no one is certain. So far Earth's scientists have discovered no signals from space that might come from extraterrestrial civilizations. Because the development of life is so long and complex, there is little chance of its being similarly produced on two worlds.

2.   We take some things for granted. For example, individual forks, knives, and plates were once considered a luxury. American settlers in the 1700s prioritized obtaining food over how to eat it. Most shared a serving utensil and a communal cup, dipped their bread into shared food, and used their fingers to eat. In the late 1800s, during the rise of the American middle class, owning full sets of tableware became a status symbol. This trend was started more than 100 years earlier by European royalty who went from spearing shared hunks of meat with pointed knives to using individual forks, knives, and plates.

3.   "I'm very concerned about Bianca, dear," Mr. Sanchez said to his wife. "As you know, her teacher says that she's much too quiet. She never participates in class discussions, and she prefers to work alone rather than in groups."

Mrs. Sanchez looked up from the book she was reading and smiled wryly. "Well," she responded, "that's true enough, Dario. But I think I know why. I can remember when my grandmother used to say the apple never falls far from the tree."

4.   "I'm not bored. Really, I'm not," said Jeremy.

"Then why did you yawn? Are you tired?" asked Tanisha.

"Just a little. But people often yawn when their body is not breathing deeply enough. In the base of our brains, we have a respiratory center that checks on the carbon dioxide in our blood. When we breathe too slowly, the center speeds up our breathing and stimulates an automatic yawn that forces us to take a deep breath. This removes the carbon dioxide," explained Jeremy.

"Now you have me yawning," said Tanisha.

"Try breathing deeply," answered Jeremy.

5.   Mr. Spiva gripped the car's wheel tightly. For many weeks he had been taking driving lessons. Now as he prepared to take his final driving test, he wondered if he would pass. Turning the wheel sharply, he pressed the accelerator pedal and lurched into traffic.

Twenty minutes later, Mr. Spiva managed to work his way into a parking space. He smiled at the examiner sitting next to him. "How did I do?" he asked the perspiring woman, who smiled back at him weakly.

	T	F	I
1. (A) Scientists say there could be life elsewhere in the universe.	☐	☐	☐
(B) Any beings elsewhere in the universe are not going to look like humans.	☐	☐	☐
(C) There have been many signals from space that might have come from extraterrestrial civilizations.	☐	☐	☐
(D) Life's path of development is long and complex.	☐	☐	☐

	T	F	I
2. (A) American settlers shared utensils and cups.	☐	☐	☐
(B) Early settlers were not wealthy enough to own full sets of tableware.	☐	☐	☐
(C) European royalty were the first to have individual forks, knives, and spoons.	☐	☐	☐
(D) The new American middle class ate with their fingers.	☐	☐	☐

	T	F	I
3. (A) Mrs. Sanchez believes that Mr. Sanchez once had the same problem Bianca has.	☐	☐	☐
(B) Mr. Sanchez is not concerned about how Bianca performs in school.	☐	☐	☐
(C) Mrs. Sanchez was reading a book.	☐	☐	☐
(D) Bianca prefers to work in groups with other children.	☐	☐	☐

	T	F	I
4. (A) Some people interpret yawning as a sign of boredom.	☐	☐	☐
(B) The human respiratory center is at the base of the brain.	☐	☐	☐
(C) Jeremy thinks you can prevent yawning by breathing deeply.	☐	☐	☐
(D) The respiratory center checks on the iron in our blood.	☐	☐	☐

	T	F	I
5. (A) Mr. Spiva did not pass the driving exam.	☐	☐	☐
(B) The examiner was perspiring.	☐	☐	☐
(C) Mr. Spiva drove smoothly throughout the exam.	☐	☐	☐
(D) The examiner had been concerned about getting into an accident.	☐	☐	☐

1. "Wilt the Stilt" was what some people called Wilt Chamberlain. This famous basketball player was once as well known as Michael Jordan. He was more than seven feet tall and still ranks as one of the best offensive players of all time. After college he played with the Harlem Globetrotters. Then he joined the now defunct Philadelphia Warriors. He played next for the Philadelphia 76ers, helping that team win the NBA title in 1967. Wilt ended his career playing with the Los Angeles Lakers, leading that team to an NBA championship in 1972. He held numerous records, including being the first NBA player to exceed 30,000 points.

2. Lawana and her father had taken the things they needed: camera, extra film, and sandwiches. Both of them knew a lot about the animals that lived in the forest and were especially good at recognizing animal tracks. "Look over here, Lawana," whispered her father when they entered the forest. "I think these tracks belong to a fox."

   Lawana looked down to see the prints in the soft, wet earth. "Yes," she said, "let's follow them."

3. Hyoun Lee had lived in the city for five years. Colin, the first neighbor he had met when he arrived, was still his best friend. The boys had many things in common, including a love of skateboarding.

   "Hey, Colin, I'll beat you to the fountain in the middle of the park," challenged Hyoun.

   "Finally, my big chance," said Colin with an impish grin. "I'm bound to win with my new skateboard."

   "Don't count on it," shouted Hyoun as he pushed off.

4. For the first time in months at sea, Stacy gave in to a feeling of homesickness. The ship was anchored offshore near a sailing village that reminded her of the coastline near her home. Because she had practically grown up on a boat, it had seemed natural for her to choose a nautical career. Now, though, her view of wharves and yachts was limited to what she could see through a periscope. But, she reminded herself, it had been her choice. Straightening, she gave the order to lower the periscope.

5. "What comes to mind when you hear 'goliath bird-eating spider'?" asked Tatsu.

   "I think of a big, hairy spider that eats birds," said Jeff.

   "You are mostly right," said Tatsu. "The goliath bird-eating spider is the largest spider in the world. The female's body grows up to four inches, and her legs can extend up to 11 inches. They are nocturnal, resting in stones and vegetation during the day. They come out at night to hunt snakes, lizards, and frogs but rarely birds."

   "Will I see one soon?" asked Jeff.

   "Not in the wild," answered Tatsu. "They live in South America."

	T	F	I

1. **(A)** Wilt Chamberlain skipped college. □ □ □
   (B) Wilt's nickname likely refers to his height. □ □ □
   (C) The Los Angeles Lakers won the NBA championship in 1972. □ □ □
   (D) Wilt Chamberlain drew attention to the sport of basketball. □ □ □

	T	F	I

2. **(A)** Lawana and her father had taken sandwiches with them. □ □ □
   (B) Lawana suggested they follow the footprints her father had spotted. □ □ □
   (C) Lawana thought the tracks belonged to a deer. □ □ □
   (D) It had rained recently. □ □ □

	T	F	I

3. **(A)** Colin had a new skateboard. □ □ □
   (B) Colin had moved to the city a year ago. □ □ □
   (C) Hyoun usually wins the skateboard races. □ □ □
   (D) Colin and Hyoun are friends. □ □ □

	T	F	I

4. **(A)** Stacy saw her hometown through the periscope. □ □ □
   (B) Stacy had often been on a boat prior to choosing a nautical career. □ □ □
   (C) Stacy is a naval officer on a submarine. □ □ □
   (D) Stacy was feeling homesick. □ □ □

	T	F	I

5. **(A)** Female goliath bird-eating spiders' bodies can grow up to eight inches. □ □ □
   (B) Goliath bird-eating spiders live in South America. □ □ □
   (C) Tatsu does not live in South America. □ □ □
   (D) Goliath bird-eating spiders eat mainly birds. □ □ □

1. "Come on! Will you move it?" Mr. Williams shouted out his car window. Then he honked his horn at the car ahead. Again he yelled out his window. "Can't you see you're holding up traffic?"

Then Mr. Williams saw what the problem was. A big, blue car was broken down in front of the car ahead of him. Mr. Williams was ashamed he had honked and yelled. He got out and helped push the stalled car to the side of the road.

2. Mrs. Ortega slapped vehemently at another mosquito. "Why aren't these annoying little insects bothering you at all?" she asked. As Mrs. Ortega scratched an itchy bump on the back of her neck, she looked at Mrs. Takeshi.

"I thought you had already put on some of this at home," said Mrs. Takeshi. "I'm sorry I didn't give this to you earlier." She handed Mrs. Ortega a plastic bottle.

"Well, I guess that's my answer," said Mrs. Ortega. "Insect repellent."

3. "I just saw a star fall right out of the sky," said Kohana.

"That's impossible," said Tionna. "Stars are millions of miles away. You couldn't have seen anything of the sort."

"Wait a second. I don't want you two to start arguing again. Let me explain," said Mr. Lopez. "What Kohana saw is sometimes called a shooting star because that's what it looks like. It's also called a meteor. Meteors are just chunks of rock from space. When they come into the air above Earth, they heat up and glow."

4. "I heard that Eric is hiding something important in his desk," whispered Emily.

"I'd like to find out what he really does have in that desk of his," said Dan.

After class, when everyone had left, Emily and Dan crept quietly to Eric's desk. Dan held open the top while Emily peeked inside. "All that's in there is a pile of books," said Emily.

Just then, the teacher walked in. "What do you children think you're doing looking in someone else's desk?" she asked angrily.

5. "I don't care at all for Philip Davis," said Theo. "All he talks about is himself."

"That's been my opinion of him too," said Charo. "He's very arrogant."

Just then Philip Davis came along. "That really is a good-looking shirt you're wearing," Philip told Theo. "Where do you get your clothes?"

As Theo answered the question, he was not certain that he disliked Philip Davis anymore.

Charo stood there with her mouth open in amazement. *Was this the same Philip Davis they had just talked about,* she wondered.

Unit 12

		T	F	I
1.	**(A)** The driver in front of Mr. Williams was not able to move.	☐	☐	☐
	(B) The driver of the stalled car did not allow Mr. Williams to help.	☐	☐	☐
	(C) The car that had stalled was blue.	☐	☐	☐
	(D) Mr. Williams would apologize to the driver of the car directly ahead of him for honking and yelling.	☐	☐	☐

		T	F	I
2.	**(A)** Mrs. Takeshi refused to give Mrs. Ortega the bottle of repellent.	☐	☐	☐
	(B) Mrs. Ortega scratched an itchy bump on the back of her neck.	☐	☐	☐
	(C) Mrs. Ortega couldn't understand why the mosquitoes were bothering only her.	☐	☐	☐
	(D) Mrs. Ortega was glad that Mrs. Takeshi had brought insect repellent along.	☐	☐	☐

		T	F	I
3.	**(A)** Mr. Lopez didn't want Kohana and Tionna to argue.	☐	☐	☐
	(B) Tionna and Kohana already knew what meteors are.	☐	☐	☐
	(C) Kohana didn't actually see a star fall from the sky.	☐	☐	☐
	(D) Tionna and Kohana often argue about different things.	☐	☐	☐

		T	F	I
4.	**(A)** Emily and Dan searched Eric's locker.	☐	☐	☐
	(B) Emily and Dan found only books in Eric's desk.	☐	☐	☐
	(C) Emily and Dan didn't want anyone to see them peek into Eric's desk.	☐	☐	☐
	(D) The teacher didn't notice that Emily and Dan were looking into Eric's desk.	☐	☐	☐

		T	F	I
5.	**(A)** Initially, Theo and Charo agreed that Philip Davis was soft-spoken and considerate of others.	☐	☐	☐
	(B) Philip complimented Theo on his shirt.	☐	☐	☐
	(C) Philip Davis was trying to change his image.	☐	☐	☐
	(D) Charo's mouth was open in amazement.	☐	☐	☐

"I'm very concerned about Bianca, dear," Mr. Sanchez said to his wife. "As you know, her teacher says that she's much too quiet. She never participates in class discussions, and she prefers to work alone rather than in groups."

Mrs. Sanchez looked up from the book she was reading and smiled wryly. "Well," she responded, "that's true enough, Dario. But I think I know why. I can remember when my grandmother used to say the apple never falls far from the tree."

A. Exercising Your Skill

The passage above lets you know that Bianca is a shy person. The word *shy* isn't used, but phrases like "much too quiet," "never participates in class discussions," and "prefers to work alone rather than in groups" give you plenty of clues as to her personality. Stories often tell about a character's personality through descriptive words and by letting you know how the character responds in different situations. Practice identifying these types of clues. For each situation below, think of how a shy person would probably act and how an outgoing person would probably act. In your answers, you can include what they would say as well as what they would do.

- Walking into a new classroom on the first day in a new school
  A shy person would probably . . .   An outgoing person would probably . . .

- Meeting someone he or she has admired for a long time
  A shy person would probably . . .   An outgoing person would probably . . .

- Accepting an award in front of a large audience
  A shy person would probably . . .   An outgoing person would probably . . .

- Responding to a teacher's request for volunteers to work on the class play
  A shy person would probably . . .   An outgoing person would probably . . .

B. Expanding Your Skill

On your paper, create word webs for *shy* and *outgoing*. Choose words from the box that relate to *shy* or to *outgoing,* and write them on the webs on your paper. You may want to start your webs like the ones below. After you have used the words in the box, add other words that you know.

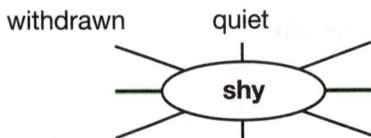

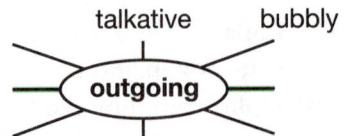

withdrawn   quiet   talkative   bubbly

shy   **outgoing**

bashful	self-confident	wary	adventurous	controlled
bold	sheepish	brave	modest	self-assured
timid	courageous	easily frightened	daring	reserved

C. Exploring Language

Read the following situations. Choose one of them, and continue it. Or if you prefer, develop a situation on your own. Include indirect suggestions in your story as well as directly stated information about the main character's personality. Write the story on your paper.

Before you begin to write, you may want to list your ideas for the story as follows:

Main idea: _____

Stated character details: _____ _____ _____

Suggested character details: _____ _____ _____

Conclusion: _____

Situations

- "We are now going to form groups to do research for our 'Foods of Different Cultures' project," announced Miss Gaines.

  Oh, no, moaned Adam to himself. *It's so awful not knowing anyone yet. I hate being a new student.* Adam lowered his eyes and prepared for the worst.

- "Now," said the master of ceremonies at Junior Musicians' Night, "do we have any junior musicians in the audience who want to show us their stuff?"

  Boy! Am I glad I brought my trumpet! thought Emma as she jumped out of her seat.

D. Expressing Yourself

Choose one of these activities.

1. With a group of classmates, think of a story everyone has read. Then think of another story in which the main character was a very different kind of person from the main character in the first story. Orally compare and contrast the two characters. Give examples of dialogue and actions that tell about their personalities. Then retell each story with the main characters switched. Show how each story and its conclusion would change.

2. With a partner pantomime different personality traits, qualities, or moods: *shy, outgoing, angry, friendly, grumpy, snobby,* and so forth. Have your classmates guess each trait after you have mimed it.

1.   "Well, there go the lights," said Uncle Thomas. "It was bound to happen sooner or later in a windstorm like this."

"I'm hungry. Let's cook something on the stove while we're waiting for the lights to come back on," suggested Tia.

"The stove is electric," said Uncle Thomas. "All the electricity is out."

"We can get food from the refrigerator," said Tia.

"The refrigerator runs on electricity too," said Uncle Thomas. "We'd better not open the door, or the cold air will escape."

"I don't like not having electricity," moaned Tia.

Just then the lights came back on.

2.   "Why do you think people started making buildings taller in northeastern cities in the early 1900s?" asked Mr. Herrera.

"Didn't a lot of people move to the cities to find jobs around that time?" ventured Pete.

"Yes," responded Mr. Herrera, "and as the cities got more crowded, more room was needed. Expansion then took place in the only direction that was left—up." The teacher continued, "Can you think of how the mass production of steel around that time added to the growth of tall buildings?"

3.   "I don't believe in things that haven't been proven to exist," said Sydney. "You can believe in flying saucers, but I think it's silly."

"Wait!" advised Mi-Ling. "The fact that a thing hasn't been proven doesn't mean that it can't exist. Before there were microscopes, nobody thought thousands of tiny animals were in a drop of pond water."

"That may be true," agreed Sydney, "but many people have believed in things that never have existed and never will. Look at the hoaxes that have fooled millions of people. I can't be tricked."

4.   "Minh didn't exaggerate when he said the hurricane did enormous damage," said Karen. "Look at those cars that were destroyed by falling trees. Dozens of homes were damaged too."

"Yes," said Julia, "the hurricane was destructive, but when I think of how that radio announcer scared us just before the storm hit, I shudder. At least there were no serious injuries or deaths."

5.   "They don't make them like this anymore," said Rico as he ran his hand along the side of his car. "Everything on it is original, from the fenders to the paint job."

"Yes, it's a beauty indeed," agreed Natalie.

"Would you like a ride?" asked Rico.

"Well," said Natalie, "are you sure it's safe?"

"Safe?" Rico looked puzzled. "Of course it's safe. Just look at it."

Natalie glanced nervously at the car. "I'd love a ride, Rico," she said, "but I'm afraid I'll be late for dinner if I take one now."

		T	F	I
1.	(A) Tia didn't know the stove was run by electricity.	☐	☐	☐
	(B) The electricity was off for many hours.	☐	☐	☐
	(C) Uncle Thomas didn't want cold air to escape from the refrigerator.	☐	☐	☐
	(D) The lights went out during a snowstorm.	☐	☐	☐

		T	F	I
2.	(A) There were already a lot of buildings in cities by the early 1900s.	☐	☐	☐
	(B) In the 1900s, many people moved to northeastern cities to find jobs.	☐	☐	☐
	(C) Cities were not very crowded in the 1900s.	☐	☐	☐
	(D) Steel was mass-produced in the early 1900s.	☐	☐	☐

		T	F	I
3.	(A) Mi-Ling believes that someday scientists will prove that flying saucers do exist.	☐	☐	☐
	(B) Sydney pointed out that hoaxes have fooled millions of people.	☐	☐	☐
	(C) Before microscopes, people knew about the tiny animals that live in drops of pond water.	☐	☐	☐
	(D) Sydney thinks it's silly to believe in flying saucers.	☐	☐	☐

		T	F	I
4.	(A) Minh didn't exaggerate about the hurricane damage.	☐	☐	☐
	(B) Karen said dozens of homes had been damaged.	☐	☐	☐
	(C) Trees had not fallen on any cars.	☐	☐	☐
	(D) The radio announcer had predicted that the storm would be much more severe than it turned out to be.	☐	☐	☐

		T	F	I
5.	(A) Rico's car was probably an antique.	☐	☐	☐
	(B) Natalie made an excuse because she had doubts about the car's safety.	☐	☐	☐
	(C) Rico invited Natalie to go for a ride in his car.	☐	☐	☐
	(D) Natalie said she was afraid of being late for her doctor's appointment.	☐	☐	☐

1.   Dylan looked at his new watch as it beeped a warning. Kylie would be late again. He studied the silver watch and reset the alarm. He checked its calendar again. Dylan was proud of that watch. It would have gotten him to the movie on time if he hadn't arranged to meet Kylie. He loved murder mysteries. Dylan stared at the watch, counting the seconds. When Kylie arrived, he'd be able to tell her exactly how late she was.

And then, there she was. "Right on time," she said as the very accurate clock in the church tower began to chime.

---

2.   Kendra was almost two years old, and her brother Tyree was five. Their playroom was closed off with a latched, folding gate that the manufacturer had labeled "childproof." This let their mother work in the kitchen and still see what was going on in the playroom. One day she went to the basement to transfer the wash to the dryer. When she returned to the kitchen, she found Kendra sitting on the kitchen floor playing with the cat. Tyree was sitting at the table, eating a banana.

---

3.   Mrs. Delgado, the school superintendent, sat in her office and watched the snowflakes swirling around in the blustery wind. In the past hour the snowfall had become heavier, and the school playground was now buried under four inches. She now had to decide whether or not to close the schools early. Were the roads going to be safe for the buses to travel on, or were they becoming impassable? *There's only one way to find out,* she thought as she reached for the telephone.

---

4. Dear Alfie,

I am 13 years old. Abby has been my best friend for five years. This year, however, we seem to have developed a lot of differences. For instance, I want to have other friends in addition to Abby. She wants to stay "just the two of us." I feel guilty. What do you suggest?
(signed) Confused

---

5.   Paulina had just come from Poland where she had lived all of her life. To help the family who hosted her in the United States, she decided to buy some groceries. She knew they needed toothpaste, but when she found the large section devoted only to toothpaste in the store, she was confused. Some tubes contained baking soda with whiteners. Some listed a mouthwash ingredient for fresh breath. Others came in orange or mint gel. Some were for sensitive teeth and gums, and others featured extra cavity protection and a combination of features. It was quite an eye opener. Making a decision would be complicated.

Unit 14

	T	F	I

1. **(A)** Dylan's watch was silver. ☐ ☐ ☐
   (B) Dylan was proud of his watch. ☐ ☐ ☐
   (C) Kylie was early. ☐ ☐ ☐
   (D) Dylan and Kylie often went places together. ☐ ☐ ☐

	T	F	I

2. **(A)** The children's mother went to the basement. ☐ ☐ ☐
   (B) The gate was not really "childproof." ☐ ☐ ☐
   (C) Tyree is younger than Kendra. ☐ ☐ ☐
   (D) The children had managed to unlock the gate. ☐ ☐ ☐

	T	F	I

3. **(A)** The snowfall had decreased in the past hour. ☐ ☐ ☐
   (B) Mrs. Delgado watched the snow falling from her office. ☐ ☐ ☐
   (C) There were four inches of snow on the playground. ☐ ☐ ☐
   (D) Mrs. Delgado would call the bus company. ☐ ☐ ☐

	T	F	I

4. **(A)** The writer feels guilty and confused. ☐ ☐ ☐
   (B) The writer wants to have other friends. ☐ ☐ ☐
   (C) Abby and the writer just met this year. ☐ ☐ ☐
   (D) Abby is jealous of the writer's other friends. ☐ ☐ ☐

	T	F	I

5. **(A)** Poland has toothpaste but fewer types to choose from. ☐ ☐ ☐
   (B) Paulina was staying with her own family. ☐ ☐ ☐
   (C) Some toothpaste types list a mouthwash ingredient for freshening breath. ☐ ☐ ☐
   (D) Paulina was somewhat overwhelmed by the choices. ☐ ☐ ☐

1. Hundreds of fans had turned out for what was to be John Peters' last performance. Singing the role he made famous nearly 50 years ago, Peters faltered only slightly on the extended notes. At the end of the performance, Peters received a standing ovation from his loyal fans—a tribute to a career that had spanned several generations. Later, one critic would sum up the feeling of most people who had attended: "At least he sang with gusto."

---

2. Trevor gnashed his teeth as he sat behind the wheel of his bright red sports car. His fingers played a drumbeat on the leather-covered steering wheel, and his feet tapped a nervous rhythm on the plush, custom-made carpeting. He thought about honking his horn but realized how useless that would be; cars were lined up on the highway as far as the eye could see. He pushed the radio buttons one after another, unable to find a song to his liking. *It will be hours before I get home,* he thought disgustedly.

---

3. Can you imagine gardens that never need watering? The early Aztec people built such gardens. The Aztecs settled on a small island in the middle of a lake. To survive, they wove reed mats, covered them with soil, and planted seeds in the soil. They placed these sprouting mats on the lake to create floating gardens—with a continuous supply of water!

---

4. Despairingly, Sonia eyed the stack of dirty dishes piled on the kitchen counter. It was her turn to clean up, but she couldn't seem to motivate herself. Sighing, Sonia looked out the window at the falling leaves. Although her mother had asked her to rake the lawn, Sonia had decided it made no sense to rake leaves until all the trees were bare. "After all," she said, "why do the same job twice?" Sonia sighed again as she remembered her mother's disapproving look.
"You think of an excuse for everything," her mother had scolded.

---

5. Nobody would ever describe Nellie Bly as meek and demure. Born as Elizabeth Cochrane, she was a journalist who wrote under the name Nellie Bly. Her articles dealt head-on with the issues of the time. After taking a job with the *New York World,* she pretended to be ill in order to be admitted to a special New York City hospital. After being released, she wrote a searing report exposing the horrific treatment and poor conditions faced by people kept in the hospital. She published a book in 1888 that helped bring about major health care reform in the United States.

Unit 15

		T	F	I
1.	(A) John Peters' voice was not what it used to be.	☐	☐	☐
	(B) As his farewell concert ended, Peters was honored by the audience.	☐	☐	☐
	(C) Only a few fans attended the last performance of John Peters.	☐	☐	☐
	(D) John Peters sang the role that he had made famous.	☐	☐	☐

		T	F	I
2.	(A) Trevor's sports car was red.	☐	☐	☐
	(B) Trevor began to honk his horn.	☐	☐	☐
	(C) Trevor was an impatient person.	☐	☐	☐
	(D) Many cars were lined up on the highway in front of Trevor.	☐	☐	☐

		T	F	I
3.	(A) Seeds were planted on reed mats that were then floated on the lake.	☐	☐	☐
	(B) The early Aztecs were determined to stay on their new island home.	☐	☐	☐
	(C) The early Aztecs knew nothing about gardening.	☐	☐	☐
	(D) Aztec people preferred to live far from water.	☐	☐	☐

		T	F	I
4.	(A) It was springtime.	☐	☐	☐
	(B) Sonia had decided to wait until all the leaves were off the trees.	☐	☐	☐
	(C) There were dirty dishes on the kitchen counter.	☐	☐	☐
	(D) Sonia doesn't enjoy doing chores around the house.	☐	☐	☐

		T	F	I
5.	(A) Nellie Bly was a pen name for Elizabeth Cochrane.	☐	☐	☐
	(B) Nellie Bly was never released from the hospital.	☐	☐	☐
	(C) Nellie Bly, as an investigative journalist, was ahead of her time.	☐	☐	☐
	(D) *New York World* was a newspaper.	☐	☐	☐

1.   "Do you know where my coat is?" Jasmine asked her mother. "I need to find it—and fast."

"What's the big rush?" asked Mrs. Glover. "Do you have plans?"

"No, but I've got to be out of the house by three," answered Jasmine, "when Malik starts practicing his trumpet."

"Well, you could come out and sit on the porch as I do. The sound is not as blaring out there," suggested Mrs. Glover.

"No, I would rather stay away altogether," said Jasmine.

2.   All night Nicole couldn't sleep. By morning she felt twice as tired as before she had gone to bed. "This is ridiculous," Nicole mumbled half aloud. "I'll just get it over with."

When Nicole got to school, she went straight to her friend Lorraine. "I want to apologize for losing my temper yesterday," said Nicole. "I was having a bad day. I didn't mean to take it out on you."

"Oh, don't give it another thought," said Lorraine. "I had already forgotten the whole incident."

3.   "Raz has been good and quiet all morning," said Mrs. Sato with a puzzled look on her face. "Do you think he's sick?"

Toru laughed. "I know why he's not barking and misbehaving. He recalls our big dinner last night and is hoping to get leftovers."

"Nonsense," said Mrs. Sato, smiling. "Raz doesn't remember there are leftovers. Sometimes he doesn't even remember his own name when we call him. Well, let's feed him anyway."

After Raz had finished eating the leftovers, he began barking and acting up like his old self.

4.   Mr. Perez stood in front of the well-stocked rack, looking at magazines. He looked through several and then put them back.

Mr. Corbett, the owner of the store, said, "Hey, are you going to buy magazines, or are you just going to stand there and read them? Tell me, would you like a chair?"

Mr. Perez stared angrily at Mr. Corbett. "I was trying to decide which magazines to buy." Mr. Perez's face grew red with anger. "Mr. Corbett, I've spent plenty of money in your store through the years, but I have made my last purchase here."

5.   "Did everybody do the homework last night?" asked Mr. Martinez.

"Yes," answered all the students.

"Then, Sally, perhaps you can answer the first question."

"I didn't understand the question," said Sally. "I didn't know how to answer it."

"Did you answer the second question?" asked Mr. Martinez.

Sally shook her head.

"In that case, you didn't do the homework," said Mr. Martinez. "I only assigned two questions."

		T	F	I
1.	(A) Mrs. Glover suggested that Jasmine sit on the porch.	☐	☐	☐
	(B) Malik maintains an unfailing practice schedule.	☐	☐	☐
	(C) Jasmine planned to attend a party at three.	☐	☐	☐
	(D) Mrs. Glover hears Malik's playing from the porch.	☐	☐	☐

		T	F	I
2.	(A) Nicole had trouble sleeping because she had mistreated her friend.	☐	☐	☐
	(B) Nicole apologized to Lorraine for losing her temper.	☐	☐	☐
	(C) Lorraine doesn't hold grudges.	☐	☐	☐
	(D) Nicole waited until after school was over to apologize to Lorraine.	☐	☐	☐

		T	F	I
3.	(A) Raz is not always a good dog.	☐	☐	☐
	(B) Toru said he knew why Raz wasn't barking and misbehaving.	☐	☐	☐
	(C) Mrs. Sato wondered if Raz might be sick.	☐	☐	☐
	(D) Raz did not eat the leftovers.	☐	☐	☐

		T	F	I
4.	(A) Mr. Perez would advise his friends not to patronize Mr. Corbett's store.	☐	☐	☐
	(B) Mr. Corbett's remarks angered Mr. Perez.	☐	☐	☐
	(C) Mr. Corbett's magazine store was poorly stocked.	☐	☐	☐
	(D) Mr. Perez would storm out of the store without buying anything.	☐	☐	☐

		T	F	I
5.	(A) Sally didn't want to admit that she hadn't done the assignment.	☐	☐	☐
	(B) All the children in the class said they had done their homework.	☐	☐	☐
	(C) Sally had completed the homework assignment.	☐	☐	☐
	(D) Sally was lying when she said she didn't understand the question.	☐	☐	☐

1. "I've known Jamal for years, but I've never seen him so upset," said Tom, looking unhappily at Carlos across the table. "He didn't even finish his sandwich."

"Try to forget it," said Carlos consolingly. "You know Jamal. He has a hot temper, but he cools off quickly."

"Just the same, I think I'll apologize." Tom scrambled out of his chair and took off in hot pursuit of his friend.

2. Propped up against the bed pillows, Benito stared thoughtfully at the playing cards in his hand. "Which one should I discard?" he mumbled, fingering one card, then another.

"Come on," said his friend Ping, sitting cross-legged at the end of the bed. "Just because you're sick doesn't mean you can take all day."

"But I want to make sure I pick the right one," insisted Benito.

"That will be the day," replied Ping.

3. Standing in the doorway of his sister's room, Diego looked distastefully at the clutter. "When are you going to clean up this mess?" he asked.

Maria, sitting in the center of the floor amid scattered magazines, stared at her brother in mock outrage. "How can you say that?" she said. "My room is a model of efficiency."

Diego refused to be put off. "I don't see how you can find anything," he persisted. "This place looks like a disaster area."

"To each his own," replied Maria.

4. Peter Wong remained outwardly calm, but inside he was bubbling with excitement. "I can't believe we're finally on our way!" he said to his younger brother, gazing with wonder at the strange countryside whizzing past the train window.

Lin Wong was young enough to be unembarrassed by displays of emotion. His small face was radiant.

"Just think," he chattered. "We'll get to eat in a good restaurant, and we'll each have a bedroom!"

5. Marta had wanted a dog of her own for a long time. Now that her family had moved to a new house with a small backyard, she had finally gotten her wish. Her parents had given her a delightful black puppy.

"Have you thought of a name yet, Marta?" asked her friend Francisca.

"Not yet," answered Marta. "Nothing seems just right."

But it didn't take long before Marta knew what to name her puppy.

"Your name has to be Digger!" shrieked Marta, as she looked at her mother's flower garden.

		T	F	I
1.	(A) Jamal didn't finish eating his sandwich.	☐	☐	☐
	(B) Tom and Jamal had just met.	☐	☐	☐
	(C) Tom left to apologize to Jamal.	☐	☐	☐
	(D) Jamal will not be upset with Tom for long.	☐	☐	☐

		T	F	I
2.	(A) Ping was sick in bed.	☐	☐	☐
	(B) Ping does not consider Benito to be a good card player.	☐	☐	☐
	(C) Ping sat at the end of the bed with his legs crossed.	☐	☐	☐
	(D) Benito finds it hard to make decisions.	☐	☐	☐

		T	F	I
3.	(A) Diego told Maria her room was a mess.	☐	☐	☐
	(B) The magazines were stacked neatly in a corner.	☐	☐	☐
	(C) Maria didn't let Diego's remarks bother her.	☐	☐	☐
	(D) Maria was asleep when Diego looked in her room.	☐	☐	☐

		T	F	I
4.	(A) Lin and Peter Wong saw unfamiliar scenery.	☐	☐	☐
	(B) The brothers will be having new experiences.	☐	☐	☐
	(C) Both boys were excited about the trip.	☐	☐	☐
	(D) Lin is Peter's older brother.	☐	☐	☐

		T	F	I
5.	(A) Marta's puppy has destroyed the flower garden.	☐	☐	☐
	(B) Francisca thought of the name for Marta's puppy.	☐	☐	☐
	(C) The dog was a gift to Marta.	☐	☐	☐
	(D) Marta's puppy had brown and white spots.	☐	☐	☐

1.   Diego's younger brother wondered if butterflies were considered different from moths because of their bright colors. Diego didn't know, so he decided to find out. He learned that moths and butterflies belong to the Lepidoptera order. **Lepidoptera** means "scaly wings," a feature of both insects. When butterflies rest, they hold their wings straight above them. Moths rest with wings flat on each side of their bodies. Diego remembered seeing moths flying near their outdoor light at night. They are nocturnal whereas butterflies are active during the day. Both insects have sensitive feelers called antennae. The antennae on each have different characteristics however.

2.   Mrs. Yang spoke with Jane about what to do with her dogs while on vacation. Mrs. Yang avoided using kennels and had previously had Jane walk her pets when she worked late. This summer Mrs. Yang would be away for ten days. She praised Jane for her dedication and knew that Jane would give her dogs the necessary play time. Jane had been thinking about how to earn money, and this conversation sparked an idea. Almost everyone in her neighborhood had some type of pet. Pet sitting wasn't a new concept, but could there be a need for it in her community?

3.   "You can tell how much snow fell in these woods last winter by looking at the pine trees," said Mr. Winkler. "Notice that all the needles are nibbled off the pines from about three feet above the ground to about eight feet. Deer have eaten those needles."

    "I see," said Paige. "The bare parts of the branches show how low and how high the deer have nibbled off the needles."

4.   "I've got some bad news," Paul solemnly told his mom and dad. "The clock in the hall doesn't work anymore."

    "It was working fine earlier," said his mom. "What happened?"

    "Well," said Paul, as he shifted from one foot to the other, "it doesn't work now because it's in pieces."

    "In pieces?" said his dad anxiously. "Did it fall off the shelf?"

    "Not exactly," said Paul, his voice quivering. He hung his head and stared at the floor. "I took it apart because I wanted to see how it worked . . . and now I can't get it back together."

5.   "Look at the big red apple I found under the tree in my backyard," said Ethan.

    "Could I take a closer look at that apple?" asked Savannah.

    "Certainly," said Ethan.

    Savannah looked carefully at the apple. "I don't think you want to eat this apple."

    "Oh, and why is that?" asked Ethan.

    "See the tiny holes?" said Savannah. "Do you know what made them?"

    "No," said Ethan, taking the apple back and biting into it.

Unit 18

		T	F	I

1. **(A)** Butterflies look for food at night. □ □ □
   (B) Diego was curious, and he wanted to answer his brother. □ □ □
   (C) Butterflies and moths have scales on their wings. □ □ □
   (D) Diego told his brother what he found out. □ □ □

	T	F	I

2. **(A)** Jane was aware that pet-sitting businesses existed. □ □ □
   (B) Mrs. Yang might take her dogs with her on vacation. □ □ □
   (C) Jane's business idea would be limited to dogs. □ □ □
   (D) Mrs. Yang trusted Jane. □ □ □

	T	F	I

3. **(A)** Mr. Winkler explained that deer had eaten the pine needles. □ □ □
   (B) There had been three feet of snow last winter. □ □ □
   (C) Deer had eaten all the needles on the pine trees. □ □ □
   (D) Deer can't reach the needles that are more than eight feet high. □ □ □

	T	F	I

4. **(A)** Paul told his parents that he had good news. □ □ □
   (B) Paul's dad asked if the clock had fallen off the shelf. □ □ □
   (C) Paul felt upset and guilty. □ □ □
   (D) Paul's dad had taken the clock apart. □ □ □

	T	F	I

5. **(A)** Ethan ate some worms along with the apple. □ □ □
   (B) Savannah showed Ethan the holes in the apple. □ □ □
   (C) Ethan found the apple in his backyard. □ □ □
   (D) Savannah found the apple to be in perfect condition. □ □ □

1. "I don't want to see another horror movie," said Marva. "After the last one I saw, I had bad dreams for a week."

"Oh, come on!" said Julian. "You can't really be afraid of something you know isn't real."

Marva turned away and took a gruesome-looking mask of a werewolf from under her coat. Then she put it over her face. When she turned to face Julian, he let out a hair-raising scream of panic.

"Now do you understand why I don't like horror movies?" said Marva calmly.

2. "I can't seem to get to sleep," said Tina. "I just keep tossing and turning when I'm in bed. I keep thinking of all the exciting things I could be doing instead of sleeping."

"I've got an answer," said her dad. "I'm going to read a book to you."

Tina's father came into her room with a book.

"Oh, no, not that book!" said Tina. "That's the most boring book in the world."

"I know," said her dad. Then he began to read. Soon Tina was sound asleep.

3. "My uncle turns off his car whenever he has to wait in traffic or in a line. He believes it uses less gasoline," said Blair.

"That's crazy. Doesn't he know that it requires extra gas to restart his engine?" replied Karen.

"He thinks you waste more gas when you idle your car," said Blair.

"You definitely use gas, but I still think you burn more gasoline by restarting," said Karen.

"What if you have to wait for longer than ten minutes?" asked Blair.

"Okay. I get the point. I wonder how long you would have to idle to justify turning off your car?" pondered Karen.

4. "What's your name, and why are you crying?" Mika asked the little boy.

"My name is Rob, and I'm crying because I'm lost," he said. "There are so many people in this big store. I can't find my mom."

Suddenly the little boy began to smile. "There she is!" he shouted. Rob's mother had spotted her little son and was moving toward him. The little boy was very happy to see his mother.

"From now on," said Rob's mother, "you'd better hold my hand when we're in the store."

5. "I caught a garter snake!" yelled Destiny as she ran to her friend Tim.

"That's great. I've never seen a snake that wasn't in a cage," said Tim.

"Well," said Destiny, "I have one right here in this box."

Destiny set the box down on the ground and opened it. There was nothing inside.

"So where's this garter snake of yours?" asked Tim expectantly.

Then Destiny noticed a little hole in the corner of the box.

	T	**F**	**I**

1. **(A)** Marva knew beforehand that Julian would try to make her see the horror movie. ☐ ☐ ☐
(B) Julian enjoyed watching scary movies. ☐ ☐ ☐
(C) Marva took the werewolf mask from under her coat. ☐ ☐ ☐
(D) Julian thought the werewolf mask was funny. ☐ ☐ ☐

	T	**F**	**I**

2. **(A)** Tina said her dad had chosen the most boring book in the world. ☐ ☐ ☐
(B) Tina went to sleep because the book didn't interest her. ☐ ☐ ☐
(C) Tina was happy about the book her dad was going to read. ☐ ☐ ☐
(D) Her father's answer to the problem didn't work. ☐ ☐ ☐

	T	**F**	**I**

3. **(A)** Blair's uncle turns off his car engine during a wait. ☐ ☐ ☐
(B) Gas may be saved by turning off the engine for long waits. ☐ ☐ ☐
(C) Karen thinks that Blair's uncle has a good theory. ☐ ☐ ☐
(D) Blair's uncle wants to conserve gas. ☐ ☐ ☐

	T	**F**	**I**

4. **(A)** The little boy's mother was thankful to find her son. ☐ ☐ ☐
(B) The boy hadn't been holding his mother's hand before he became lost. ☐ ☐ ☐
(C) Mika asked the little boy why he was crying. ☐ ☐ ☐
(D) The little boy was sad to see his mother. ☐ ☐ ☐

	T	**F**	**I**

5. **(A)** Tim had seen snakes before, but they had been in cages. ☐ ☐ ☐
(B) Destiny said the snake she had caught was in the box. ☐ ☐ ☐
(C) The snake had escaped from the box through the little hole. ☐ ☐ ☐
(D) Destiny was afraid of snakes. ☐ ☐ ☐

"I don't want to see another horror movie," said Marva. "After the last one I saw, I had bad dreams for a week."

"Oh, come on!" said Julian. "You can't really be afraid of something you know isn't real."

Marva turned away and took a gruesome-looking mask of a werewolf from under her coat. Then she put it over her face. When she turned to face Julian, he let out a hair-raising scream of panic.

"Now do you understand why I don't like horror movies?" said Marva calmly.

A. Exercising Your Skill

In the passage above, you can guess the movie frightened Marva so much she had bad dreams for a week. You can guess Julian was probably frightened by the werewolf mask because he let out a hair-raising scream. In stories, characters act in certain ways when they have certain feelings, such as fear, anger, excitement, or boredom. Sometimes characters' feelings are described directly in a story. Other times you can guess what they are probably feeling because of what they do or because of what they say in dialogue, or conversation.

The list below tells things a person did. For each action on the list, tell what emotion the character was probably feeling, such as fear, anger, excitement, or boredom. If the behavior could suggest more than one feeling, say so.

Actions:
- frowned deeply
- chuckled quietly
- started to tremble all over
- gasped, "Wow!"
- let out a piercing wail
- felt eyelids sink like weights
- clenched fists
- yawned repeatedly
- broke out in a cold sweat
- jumped at every noise
- gritted teeth
- felt eyes open wide
- jumped up and down and clapped hands
- sat straight up in bed

B. Expanding Your Skill

For one emotion, such as surprise or grief, write several character actions like the ones above. Read your actions to a partner. Can your partner guess which emotion the actions express?

C. Exploring Language

Write and illustrate a short fairy tale storybook for young children. Decide on two characters—such as a big, friendly dragon named Donald and a light-as-a-feather sprite named Sophie. Make up a simple plot that will involve the characters in situations that can bring forth two or three emotions. Plan to reveal these emotions—such as joy, wonder, fear, and excitement—through the characters' actions and conversations rather than by describing them directly.

Illustrate each page of the book, and include three to five lines of story text on each page.

You may want to organize the information for your book in this way:

1. Characters: _____
2. Setting: _____
3. Problem: _____
   • Action: _____
   • Action: _____
   • Action: _____
4. Resolution: _____

5. Emotions Revealed by Actions and Conversations:

_____
_____
_____
_____
_____

Ask one or two classmates to read your story and to identify the emotions revealed by actions and conversations. Then give the book to a young child to read and enjoy!

D. Expressing Yourself

Choose one of these activities.

1. Pretend that you are a television reporter at the site of an exciting sports event—and history is in the making. You are on the air live and telling your audience what is happening as it happens. Try to capture the feelings of the participants and the spectators by revealing their actions rather than by describing the feelings directly. For example: "The crowd is hushed. Leah stands at the tape, reaches high over her head, and slams the ball into Nina's fair-play area. Leah lets out a whoop as she wins the set, the match, and the game!" Present your broadcast to your classmates, and see if they "catch" the mood.

2. Make up sayings for fortune cookies. Write sayings that link behavior with feelings. For example: "A smile on your face speaks louder than words" and "One who wastes time can never feel thrifty at heart." You and your classmates may want to throw your sayings into a hat and then each pick a fortune for the day.

1. Scout was lying comfortably at Mrs. Banderas's feet as she knitted in her chair. Suddenly the dog lifted its head, raised its ears, and let out a low growl.

"Easy, Scout," said Mrs. Banderas. "I thought I heard something outside too. But we're safe here in our living room. If anyone tries to break in, the police will know and be here within two minutes."

---

2. "I just read about a certain type of tree that has roots that grow downward from its branches and then take root in the soil below," said Seki.

"Really?" Kenji responded. "What kind of tree is that, and where does it grow?"

"It's the banyan tree, and it grows in India," said Seki. "I also read that sometimes there are so many roots growing down that one banyan tree can look like an entire grove!"

---

3. "Tell me I don't sound like that," said Ashley.

"Yes. You do," said Lena. The two girls were listening to a recording of Ashley giving a speech. They replayed part of it for Ashley's father. He agreed it sounded very much like Ashley's voice. Ashley was astounded and began to wonder why she heard her own voice so differently. After doing some research, she learned that people hear their own voices from sound waves transmitted through the air and through sound waves traveling through the bones in their head. Other listeners hear other people's voices only from the sound waves carried by air.

---

4. Atop the snow-covered mountain, the sign pointing to the left said "Beginner's Trail." Luandra adjusted her ski bindings and gazed down the left trail. It dropped off very steeply, and she could see several sharp, narrow turns. "Something's wrong here," she thought. "This can't be a beginner's trail. The trail to the right looks easier to me. I wonder if those snickering youngsters I saw walking away from the signpost had anything to do with this."

---

5. "I'm sorry," said the telephone operator, "but the number you have reached has been temporarily disconnected."

"But that's my own phone number!" shouted Makya.

"I'm sorry," the voice repeated, "but the number you have reached . . ."

"Ugh," moaned Makya, "a recorded message. Well, I'm going home to see why my phone isn't working."

When Makya got to his street, he saw a telephone repair truck and a police car there. A car had knocked down a telephone pole.

"When will my phone be fixed?" Makya asked the workers.

"We'll have it working again within a half hour," they answered.

Unit 20

		T	F	I
1.	**(A)** Scout is a good watchdog.	☐	☐	☐
	(B) Mrs. Banderas's home is equipped with a burglar alarm.	☐	☐	☐
	(C) Mrs. Banderas did not feel safe in the living room.	☐	☐	☐
	(D) Mrs. Banderas said the police could arrive within two minutes.	☐	☐	☐

		T	F	I
2.	**(A)** Seki learned about banyan trees from a movie.	☐	☐	☐
	(B) A single banyan tree can look like a grove.	☐	☐	☐
	(C) Banyan tree roots grow from the branches down to the soil.	☐	☐	☐
	(D) Seki and Kenji do not live in India.	☐	☐	☐

		T	F	I
3.	**(A)** The recording was of Ashley singing.	☐	☐	☐
	(B) Hearing your voice as it is carried through your bones changes the sound.	☐	☐	☐
	(C) Ashley doesn't like how her voice sounds to others.	☐	☐	☐
	(D) Voices are transmitted through the air by sound waves.	☐	☐	☐

		T	F	I
4.	**(A)** The left trail was steep and sharply curved.	☐	☐	☐
	(B) Luandra didn't detect any difference between the beginner's and the advanced trails.	☐	☐	☐
	(C) The youngsters had put the "Beginner's Trail" sign at the entrance to the advanced trail.	☐	☐	☐
	(D) Luandra didn't go down the left trail.	☐	☐	☐

		T	F	I
5.	**(A)** Makya was shouting at a recording, not a live operator.	☐	☐	☐
	(B) The workers said Makya's phone would be working again in 15 minutes.	☐	☐	☐
	(C) Makya does not have much patience.	☐	☐	☐
	(D) A telephone pole had been knocked down.	☐	☐	☐

1.   "Hey, Venus, wake up," whispered Litonya as she elbowed her friend gently.

"Uh . . . oh," mumbled Venus. "I hardly sleep at night. Mom and Dad get up for the feedings, but I just can't resist peeking at Jamil every time I hear him wake up."

"Girls, do you have something to share with us?" asked Mr. Rivera, at the board.

2.   Painters have often been able to correct a mistake with one or more brush strokes. Bette Clair Nesmith had long watched with fascination as her artist friends would paint over an error and start again. This gave Nesmith, an executive secretary, an idea. She decided to do the same thing at her office. Using a tempera water-based paint and a small brush, Nesmith began to cover her typing errors. The new product she created—correction fluid—has since become an indispensable tool in most offices and many homes.

3.   Are sloths lazy or just well adapted? Sloths are truly one of the slowest species of land animals. When they do finally decide to move, after hanging upside-down from a tree, they lug their bodies no more than six feet per minute. They live in the rain forests of Central and South America, where they slowly eat tree leaves. Their low body temperature helps them conserve energy. Sloths have a very unusual color for mammals—green. The unusual hue comes from blue-green algae growing in their hair. It helps them blend into the canopy so they can be left alone.

4.   It takes 15 to 18 years for a human's bones, which consist mainly of calcium and phosphorus, to grow and for the person to reach full height. In four to five months, a male deer's antlers, which are bony outgrowths, are complete. The antlers begin as small bumps on the frontal bones of the deer's skull. The skin, or velvet, that covers these bumps grows along with them. In late summer, when the antlers have stopped growing, the velvet dries up and falls off. At the end of the spring season, the antlers are shed and the deer grows a new set. Biologists know of no faster bone growth than that of antlers.

5.   Kyle was being watched. As he made his way through the bookstore, he stopped to look at some calendars. Then he headed over to the café, where he thumbed through his favorite magazines. Unbeknownst to Kyle, a woman was taking notes regarding his every move. Was he being watched for shoplifting? It is very likely that Kyle is being spied on for market research purposes. Many stores hire consumer-research firms to study the habits and interests of their customers. Using technology and undercover staff, they study how people move through a store, where they spend their time, and who is buying which items.

		T	F	I
1.	**(A)** Venus and Litonya are in school.	☐	☐	☐
	(B) Jamil is Venus's baby brother.	☐	☐	☐
	(C) Venus's mother and father share the feeding of Jamil.	☐	☐	☐
	(D) Venus can sleep through any kind of disturbance.	☐	☐	☐

		T	F	I
2.	**(A)** Correction fluid is used in most offices and many homes.	☐	☐	☐
	(B) A painter can often paint over an error and start again.	☐	☐	☐
	(C) Nesmith's invention is not useful.	☐	☐	☐
	(D) Nesmith made a good deal of money from her idea.	☐	☐	☐

		T	F	I
3.	**(A)** Sloths spend most of their time high in the trees.	☐	☐	☐
	(B) Sloths have green hair.	☐	☐	☐
	(C) Sloths do not need speed because of their other adaptations.	☐	☐	☐
	(D) Sloths live in Central America and South America.	☐	☐	☐

		T	F	I
4.	**(A)** The antlers of a male deer grow to full size in four to five months.	☐	☐	☐
	(B) The antlers of a deer contain the same substances found in the bones of humans.	☐	☐	☐
	(C) It takes 15 to 18 years for a person to reach full height.	☐	☐	☐
	(D) The antlers of a deer usually begin growing in late summer.	☐	☐	☐

		T	F	I
5.	**(A)** Consumer research firms focus mainly on shoplifting.	☐	☐	☐
	(B) Kyle spent time looking at magazines.	☐	☐	☐
	(C) Stores hire consumer-research firms to investigate shoppers' habits.	☐	☐	☐
	(D) The undercover researcher will discuss Kyle's shopping preferences in her report.	☐	☐	☐

1. Is a single vote important? President Thomas Jefferson was elected by only one vote in the House of Representatives. The same was true for President John Quincy Adams. Rutherford B. Hayes won the presidency by a single electoral vote. Likewise, Texas, Oregon, Washington, and Idaho were admitted into the United States by one senatorial vote each. In 1941, just before the U.S. involvement in World War II, Congress ruled—again by a single vote—to continue the Selective Service Act, drafting men into the army to keep America prepared.

2. Roshonda had been at camp for three weeks. Her favorite activity was canoeing. When the day came for her to take her canoe test, Roshonda felt confident that she would pass. She knew the strokes and could steer a canoe well. The counselor who was testing Roshonda sat in the middle of the canoe; Roshonda was in the stern. The trip started out well with Roshonda paddling strongly and in full control. But suddenly, while switching her paddle from one side to the other, she lost her grip on it. The paddle slipped and fell into the water.

3. Cousins Victoria Holley and Brandon Deans joined their parents on an outing to White Sands National Monument in New Mexico. The cousins soon kicked off their shoes to play in nature's huge "sandbox."

"White Sands covers 275 square miles," said Mrs. Deans to her sister, Mrs. Holley. "The dunes are composed of gypsum, a mineral used to make plaster of paris. What an interesting place this is!"

While the sisters chatted, Mr. Deans and Mr. Holley asked the children to race up a steep dune with them. The cousins quickly made it to the top. The fathers were only partway up when the delighted children rolled down past them at lightning speed!

4. In the 40 years they were married, Mrs. Yang and her husband had run the family business and reared their seven children. When her husband died, Mrs. Yang continued to stay in the big house, even though the children were living on their own. It was nice having a large house when the grandchildren came to visit. Mrs. Yang enjoyed her garden of flowers and vegetables and loved having her friends in for tea. But now she was 90 years old and finding it hard to keep the big house going or even to cook for herself. She had to make plans to change her way of life.

5. The great-granddaughter of Louis Wilson made the following notes: "According to the deed, Louis Wilson purchased a farm in Centerville in 1872. This was a 160-acre parcel. He married Ruth Sanders in 1877."

"Other relatives living in this area included Charles Wilson, the general contractor. In 1880 he built the courthouse."

"A Lucy Wilson also made rural land purchases here in 1883 and 1884, and a Lucy Wilson who died in 1910 is buried in the church cemetery in Centerville."

		T	F	I
1.	**(A)** One person's political vote can change history.	☐	☐	☐
	(B) Idaho was admitted into the United States by one senatorial vote.	☐	☐	☐
	(C) Jefferson, Adams, and Washington were elected president by a single vote.	☐	☐	☐
	(D) An eligible voter cannot afford to abstain from voting on Election Day.	☐	☐	☐

		T	F	I
2.	**(A)** Roshonda didn't pass her canoe test that day.	☐	☐	☐
	(B) The counselor sat in the middle of the canoe.	☐	☐	☐
	(C) Roshonda knew beforehand that she'd never pass the test.	☐	☐	☐
	(D) After the paddle slipped, Roshonda was very embarrassed.	☐	☐	☐

		T	F	I
3.	**(A)** White Sands National Monument covers 275 square miles.	☐	☐	☐
	(B) The cousins had the most fun on the outing.	☐	☐	☐
	(C) Mrs. Holley and Mrs. Deans are cousins.	☐	☐	☐
	(D) Plaster of paris is made from gypsum.	☐	☐	☐

		T	F	I
4.	**(A)** Mr. Yang outlived Mrs. Yang.	☐	☐	☐
	(B) Mrs. Yang has decided to sell the big house.	☐	☐	☐
	(C) The Yangs had been married for 40 years.	☐	☐	☐
	(D) Mrs. Yang was thinking about moving in with one of her children.	☐	☐	☐

		T	F	I
5.	**(A)** The great-granddaughter of Louis Wilson was making notes for a family tree.	☐	☐	☐
	(B) Ruth Sanders married Charles Wilson.	☐	☐	☐
	(C) The courthouse was built in 1880.	☐	☐	☐
	(D) The notes would have to be correlated with other research on the Wilsons.	☐	☐	☐

1. Professor Richard Eakin of the University of California enlivened his biology classes by impersonating famous scientists. When the renowned nineteenth-century biologist Charles Darwin was the subject, Professor Eakin would don a false beard and a frock coat and "guest-lecture" as Darwin himself might have done. To teach the findings of the priest-scientist Gregor Mendel, Eakin would appear in clerical robes. He also imitated the appearance and accent of Louis Pasteur. Eakin would spend up to three hours applying makeup for a role. He found that a scientific idea meant more to his students when the discoverer seemed to be explaining it.

2. From 1929 to 1941 a steam-powered train, *Blue Comet,* offered luxury runs between New York, New York, and Atlantic City, New Jersey. The interior and exterior of the train were mostly blue. The blue of the exterior was broken by a cream-colored stripe that ran the length of the train on both sides. The *Blue Comet* provided fast, three-hour service between the two cities. People used to line the tracks just to watch the train fly by. Everything about it suggested a speeding blue comet. Each car of the train was even named for a celestial comet. The *Blue Comet* made its final trip on September 27, 1941.

3. Sherita and her father had flown to the West Indies and were vacationing on the beach in Grand Cayman.
    "Dad, you were in the naval submarine service," said Sherita. "What is it really like to travel in a submarine?"
    "I can do better than describe what it's like," said Dad. "Believe it or not, I've arranged for the two of us to explore the undersea world around Grand Cayman tomorrow. We'll be leaving early on a 28-passenger submarine named *Atlantis.* Now you'll finally be able to see for yourself how exciting submarine travel really is."

4. "What is your favorite color?" asked Michele.
    "It used to be green, but now it's blue," said Brett.
    "You like to spend time alone, don't you? Blue and green are colors that draw people inward, and people who like cool colors are often introverts," said Michele.
    "That's interesting," said Brett. "What is your favorite color?"
    "Purple," said Michele. "People who like purple are supposed to be intuitive and imaginative."
    "I guess that describes you," said Brett. "What about red?"
    "People who like red are often passionate and full of energy. A preference for red, yellow, or orange suggests an outgoing personality," said Michele.

5. Humankind sometimes experiences terrible tragedies, then realizes that preventive safety measures could have saved countless lives. Ever since the great loss of life that resulted when the *Titanic* sank in 1912, ships must carry sufficient lifeboats and operate their radios 24 hours a day. Because 168 people were killed in a circus-tent fire in Hartford, Connecticut, in 1944, modern circus tents are made of nonflammable materials.

	T	**F**	**I**

1. **(A)** Professor Eakin taught biology in California. ☐ ☐ ☐
   (B) Professor Eakin usually dressed as a clown for his lectures. ☐ ☐ ☐
   (C) Professor Eakin was a good actor. ☐ ☐ ☐
   (D) Professor Eakin enjoyed teaching. ☐ ☐ ☐

	T	**F**	**I**

2. **(A)** It took three hours to travel from New York City to Atlantic City on the *Blue Comet.* ☐ ☐ ☐
   (B) Passengers aboard the *Blue Comet* received exceptionally fine service. ☐ ☐ ☐
   (C) The *Blue Comet* was a diesel-powered train. ☐ ☐ ☐
   (D) The seats and the carpeting of the train were mostly blue. ☐ ☐ ☐

	T	**F**	**I**

3. **(A)** Sherita's father had arranged a trip on the *Nautilus.* ☐ ☐ ☐
   (B) Jamaica is in the West Indies. ☐ ☐ ☐
   (C) Sherita has heard tales about the exciting life aboard a submarine. ☐ ☐ ☐
   (D) Sherita's father enjoyed his submarine duty of the past. ☐ ☐ ☐

	T	**F**	**I**

4. **(A)** Brett does not think Michele is imaginative or intuitive. ☐ ☐ ☐
   (B) Fans of red are supposed to be passionate. ☐ ☐ ☐
   (C) Extroverts prefer warm colors, and introverts are drawn to cool colors. ☐ ☐ ☐
   (D) Brett is considering switching his favorite color to green. ☐ ☐ ☐

	T	**F**	**I**

5. **(A)** The *Titanic* was not equipped with enough lifeboats for all its passengers. ☐ ☐ ☐
   (B) Two major disasters in 1944 occurred in the United States. ☐ ☐ ☐
   (C) A circus-tent fire in Hartford, Connecticut, killed 168 people. ☐ ☐ ☐
   (D) Important knowledge is often acquired as the result of tragedies. ☐ ☐ ☐

1. The largest and heaviest horses in the world are the great shires, weighing more than 2,000 pounds and standing as high as 18 hands (six feet) at the shoulder.

    Shires can haul heavy loads. Two shires in England pulled a world-record load for horses: 56 tons.

    In the Middle Ages, when English knights were seeking a breed of horse that would carry an armored warrior into battle, they chose the shire. In fact, the horses themselves wore armor from head to hoof.

2. "The opposing team is desperate to win," remarked Tariq. "They'll do anything, even sneak in a ringer."

    "What's a ringer?" asked Javier.

    "A top-notch player a team brings in from outside but who's not officially allowed to be on the team. Some teams try to get away with using a ringer, but it's illegal," replied Tariq.

    Just then Javier looked at the opposing team's bench and saw a huge player, more than six feet tall, with muscles almost bursting out of his uniform. "I've never seen him before," said Javier. "I wonder . . ."

3. Are you accustomed to entering your house through a door in the roof? You probably aren't, but the early Pueblo Indians were. For protection the windows of their multistoried brick dwellings were located high off the ground. Likewise, the doors were located in the roofs and could be reached only by way of removable ladders. Thus, the Pueblo Indians often "came down the door."

4. "Why are you cutting the green tops off the carrots?" Craig asked his dad.

    "Leaving them on drains their moisture," he answered. "It is also a good idea to store carrots and cucumbers in the refrigerator far from fruits."

    "Why?" asked Craig.

    "Fruits produce ethylene gas that hardens a cucumber's seeds and makes carrots bitter."

    "I didn't know fruit storage was such a science," said Craig. "What else is there to know?"

    "Potatoes should never go in the refrigerator. Cold temperatures convert their starch to sugar and change their taste and color. They keep best in dark, well-ventilated places."

5. The creature South American jungle dwellers fear most is the anaconda, a green-and-black snake that can swallow deer—whole.

    Anacondas are the largest of the boa family snakes. Determining how long they can grow involves untangling fact from legend. Explorers have claimed seeing 40-, 60-, and even 140-foot anacondas. The "official" record—still not universally accepted—is 37½ feet. A large prize offered for a 30-footer has never been claimed. But 20-footers are common.

    The anaconda kills by suffocating its prey.

		T	**F**	**I**
1.	**(A)** Shires were used as war horses during the Middle Ages.	☐	☐	☐
	(B) Two shires in England pulled 56 tons.	☐	☐	☐
	(C) Knights would try to kill an enemy knight's horse.	☐	☐	☐
	(D) Shires could not bear the weight of heavy armor.	☐	☐	☐

		T	**F**	**I**
2.	**(A)** The huge player was a ringer.	☐	☐	☐
	(B) The opposing team was cheating.	☐	☐	☐
	(C) Javier learned what a ringer is from Tariq.	☐	☐	☐
	(D) As a general rule, teams are permitted to use ringers.	☐	☐	☐

		T	**F**	**I**
3.	**(A)** Early Pueblo Indians lived in wooden frame houses.	☐	☐	☐
	(B) The dwellings of the Pueblos often had more than one level.	☐	☐	☐
	(C) The Pueblos had enemies nearby.	☐	☐	☐
	(D) Pueblo dwellings had roof-level doors.	☐	☐	☐

		T	**F**	**I**
4.	**(A)** Potatoes taste best when they are starchy, not sugary.	☐	☐	☐
	(B) Fruits emit methane gas.	☐	☐	☐
	(C) Potatoes should be stored in dark places with good ventilation.	☐	☐	☐
	(D) People prefer their carrots sweet and their cucumbers with soft seeds.	☐	☐	☐

		T	**F**	**I**
5.	**(A)** The anaconda is not a poisonous snake.	☐	☐	☐
	(B) The anaconda is the smallest member of the boa family.	☐	☐	☐
	(C) Jungle dwellers fear the anaconda more than any other creature.	☐	☐	☐
	(D) The anaconda kills by suffocating its victim.	☐	☐	☐

1.   Sergei looked forward to his first meal with his American family. An exchange student from the Ukraine, Sergei would be spending three months in the United States, learning about the country's people and their culture. At dinner Sergei was bombarded with questions from the Johnsons, especially from Jamila, the talkative eight-year-old.

    Her first question, "What is your family like?" was followed in quick succession by "Do you have a sister my age?" and "Is the weather cold in the Ukraine?" and so on.

    "Hey, Jamila," interrupted Terrez, her older brother. "Maybe Sergei would like to get a question in sometime soon?"

2.   "Amazing!" exclaimed Ariel. "You can't see the other side. It reminds me a little of the ocean, only it's much colder and the water isn't salty."

    "It is big. The states of Massachusetts, Vermont, New Hampshire, Rhode Island, and most of Connecticut could fit inside its shoreline," said Marta.

    "Look at the waves. I had no idea an inland lake could have giant waves," said Ariel.

    "Some people say it has the world's most dangerous water. More than 350 sunken boats lie on Lake Superior's bottom." explained Marta. "Violent storms come up suddenly, and boaters are in danger because they often have little warning."

3.   "Something's all wrong," muttered Raquel as she opened her eyes to the bright morning sun streaming through her bedroom window. "The sun shouldn't be up. It's the middle of January, and my alarm clock says 6:30 A.M. It should still be dark outside."

    Raquel checked the clock. The numbers were lit, and the digits changed to 6:31 as she watched. The clock definitely was working. But from the avenue she heard sounds of school buses, which normally don't run until after eight.

4.   Braden broke away from the defender and dribbled in for another easy score. The home-team crowd groaned. The home team was now down by seven points with two minutes to go.

    In the stands, the home crowd wondered why Coach Browne hadn't put Yusef in. Yusef not only was the team's high scorer but was at least two inches taller than anyone on the opposing team.

    Finally, the coach motioned for Yusef to go in. The crowd cheered wildly. Yusef jumped up and trotted onto the court, limping.

5.   Did Marco Polo really spend 17 years in China, or was he an armchair traveler with a powerful imagination and a way with words? His book *The Description of the World* details the gems, spices, and silk of the East. But historians who question his exploits note he never mentions the Great Wall, the many varieties of tea in China, or even chopsticks. Yet when Marco Polo visited, the Great Wall was worn down in many places, not a formidable barrier. As for eating, Marco Polo spent more time dining with other foreigners who sliced meat with knives and ate with their hands.

		T	F	I

1. **(A)** The Johnsons were hosting an exchange student from the Ukraine. □ □ □
(B) Sergei had arrived at the Johnsons' home three weeks ago. □ □ □
(C) Terrez thought Jamila was being overly nosey and rude. □ □ □
(D) Jamila was only eight years old. □ □ □

		T	F	I

2. **(A)** Ariel and Marta are discussing Lake Superior. □ □ □
(B) More than 350 sunken boats lie on the lake's bottom. □ □ □
(C) Ariel saw the ocean before and is seeing Lake Superior for the first time. □ □ □
(D) Ariel is not impressed by the body of water. □ □ □

		T	F	I

3. **(A)** When Raquel awoke, her clock indicated it was 6:30 A.M. □ □ □
(B) Raquel will be late for school. □ □ □
(C) The clock was not working correctly. □ □ □
(D) It was a cloudy day. □ □ □

		T	F	I

4. **(A)** The home team was at a disadvantage without Yusef. □ □ □
(B) Braden was on the home team. □ □ □
(C) Yusef was the team's high scorer. □ □ □
(D) The coach had kept Yusef out because of an injury. □ □ □

		T	F	I

5. **(A)** Historians have differing opinions on Marco Polo. □ □ □
(B) Marco Polo wrote a book titled *The Description of the World.* □ □ □
(C) His failure to mention important aspects of China can be explained. □ □ □
(D) The Chinese did not use chopsticks when Marco Polo visited. □ □ □

The Last L A P
Language Activity Pages

Nobody would ever describe Nellie Bly as meek and demure. Born as Elizabeth Cochrane, she was a journalist who wrote under the name Nellie Bly. Her articles dealt head-on with the issues of the time. After taking a job with the *New York World,* she pretended to be ill in order to be admitted to a special New York City hospital. After being released she wrote a searing report exposing the horrific treatment and poor conditions faced by people kept in the hospital. She published a book in 1888 that helped bring about major health care reform in the United States.

A. Exercising Your Skill

The passage above references a specific historical period. It is nonfiction. Historical fiction stories, however, tell about real or imaginary characters located in actual historical settings or taking part in real historical events. Sometimes a story states a period directly. At other times details are given that suggest or portray the time or the event.

Play an association game with a partner. One partner should read the historical detail clues below. The other partner should say what time period or event the detail *most likely* refers to. Take turns reading and relating. If neither of you can figure out what period is implied, try to find out from other people or from reference books.

Historical Detail Clues:

Pony Express	gladiators and the Colosseum
Sputnik	panhandler
blue and gray uniforms	the *Mayflower*
knights, armor, horses, jousts	prairie schooners
BASIC and LOGO	pharaohs, the Sphinx, and hieroglyphics
the Model T	the Acropolis at Athens
Johnny Appleseed	cattle drives
the Alamo	the U.S.S. *Constitution*
Squanto	Plymouth Rock
Robin Hood	Tyrannosaurus rex
Buffalo Bill Cody	

B. Expanding Your Skill

With a partner decide on one of the events or time periods indicated in Part A, and find more details about it. Then take turns telling a fictional chain story. You tell the first part, your partner tells the next part, and so on. Make sure that your story includes details suggesting the mood or circumstances of the time. Tell the story to the rest of the class. When you have finished, ask your audience if they got a "feel" for the time or event portrayed.

C. Exploring Language

Decide on one of the time periods or events listed below. Do research to find more details about it. Then write a diary entry of a character who might have lived at that time. Include details that give a sense of what the time was like without actually saying what it was like. If someone reads your entry, he or she should be able to answer questions like these, even though the information is not stated directly: *Was electric power in use at the time? What types of transportation were used then? What did people value most then—freedom, mobility, recreation, religion, or something else?*

<u>Historical Periods and Events:</u>

The settling of Colonial Jamestown
The first railroad to the American West
Everyday life in the Old Kingdom of Ancient Egypt
Incan life at Machu Picchu
Simón Bolívar acts as "The Liberator" of South America
The Boston Tea Party
Robert Scott heads for the South Pole
The Lewis and Clark Expedition
Daniel Boone helps open the Wilderness Road

D. Expressing Yourself

Choose one of these activities.

1. Illustrate a scene of daily life in a specific historical time period. Include details that suggest the time period and what life was like then on a daily basis. You may write a caption for your illustration, but do not be specific about the period. See if your classmates can guess the time period represented. Talk about what daily life must have been like then.

2. With two or three classmates, act out a scene from a well-known historical event. Use words, body movements, and facial expressions to tell about what is happening, but do not use any words that directly name the characters or the event. See how quickly your classmates can guess the event you are acting out.